Narrativizing Theories

Narrativizing Theories
An Aesthetic of Ambiguity

Benjamin John Peters

CASCADE *Books* • Eugene, Oregon

NARRATIVIZING THEORIES
An Aesthetic of Ambiguity

Copyright © 2020 Benjamin John Peters. All rights reserved. Except for brief quotations in critical publications or reviews, no part of this book may be reproduced in any manner without prior written permission from the publisher. Write: Permissions, Wipf and Stock Publishers, 199 W. 8th Ave., Suite 3, Eugene, OR 97401.

Cascade Books
An Imprint of Wipf and Stock Publishers
199 W. 8th Ave., Suite 3
Eugene, OR 97401

www.wipfandstock.com

PAPERBACK ISBN: 978-1-5326-9489-9
HARDCOVER ISBN: 978-1-5326-9490-5
EBOOK ISBN: 978-1-5326-9491-2

Cataloguing-in-Publication data:

Names: Peters, Benjamin John, author.

Title: Narrativizing theories : an aesthetic of ambiguity / by Benjamin John Peters.

Description: Eugene, OR: Cascade Books, 2020. | Includes bibliographical references.

Identifiers: ISBN 978-1-5326-9489-9 (paperback). | ISBN 978-1-5326-9490-5 (hardcover). | ISBN 978-1-5326-9491-2 (ebook).

Subjects: LCSH: Aesthetics. | Ambiguity. | Philosophy. | Theology.

Classification: BH39 P48 2020 (print). | BH39 (ebook).

Manufactured in the U.S.A.   02/03/20

To Boris and Kristin

The terrain on which philosophy and literature traditionally meet is ethics. Or, rather, ethics has always provided an excuse for philosophy and literature not to look each other directly in the face, being certain and confident of being able to reach easy agreement about their task of teaching virtue to mankind.

—Italo Calvino, *The Uses of Literature*

Contents

Introduction | ix

Part I: A Theory of Ambiguity

Chapter One: Slippery Words | 3

Chapter Two: Echoes of Ambiguity | 24

    Excursus One: *The Dispossessed* | 49

Chapter Three: Some Lines Can't Be Crossed | 57

Part II: A Narrativizing Theory

Chapter Four: The Spy and the Priest | 79

    Excursus Two: *The Kingdom* | 104

Chapter Five: Mapping the Forest | 111

Chapter Six: The Finale Is Humor | 133

    Excursus Three: *Sailing to Sarantium* | 141

Conclusion | 150

Bibliography | 153

Introduction

How we remember changes how we have lived. Time runs both ways. We make stories of our lives.

—Guy Gavriel Kay, *Under Heaven*

While I was writing about ambiguity and aesthetics in the searing, summer sun of 2017, Philip Salim Francis was busy arguing that modern aesthetic theory tends to focus, above all else, on art's capacity to disrupt. "The arts," he writes, "unsettle our entrenched ways of thinking and believing... When we are immersed in an aesthetic experience, it is argued, our conceptual, categorical, and binary ways of thinking give way."[1] This line of reasoning inevitably leads, however, to art's salvific potential, secular aesthetic religions, and the universalization of aesthetic theories. Francis recognizes this and suggests that modern aesthetic theory is "in dire need of a dose of its own historicizing medicine."[2]

I agree. Aesthetic theory assumes categorical rupture, universalizes it, and then foists it onto aesthetic experience. And yet, art also has the frightening capacity to reify beliefs and practices that are unpalatable to modern, liberal worldviews.

While Francis doesn't present a solution to this conundrum of aesthetic theory, he does, unwittingly, open a space for me to explore an aesthetic of ambiguity. Yes, disruption is only one aspect of art. But once an aesthetic experience has ruptured a category, exposing alternate though equally valid ways of moving in the world, then how does one choose between competing worldviews? "It may be," Francis writes:

> that much of the failure to understand 'fundamentalism' results from a refusal to place the structure of one's own mind in familial relation to that of one's relatively conservative cousins...

---

1. Francis, *When Art Disrupts Religion*, 4–5.
2. Francis, *When Art Disrupts Religion*, 9.

Do we not all, in our different ways, maintain certain beliefs intractably? Shouldn't we? Are not some beliefs worth *preserving*?[3]

He goes so far as to say, in fact, that some beliefs and practices are worth maintaining even amidst the defamiliarizing experience of aesthetics.[4]

The question that follows then is the question that governs much of *Narrativizing Theories*. How do we "distinguish acceptable (or ethical) methods of belief and identity preservation from the unacceptable?"[5] I answer this question, though articulated differently at times, in six chapters, three excursuses, and one short story embedded throughout the length of this book. Taken together, I argue that an aesthetic rooted in ambiguity emphasizes both the provisionality of knowledge and the narrativization of reality.

In Part I, I define ambiguity as "coexistent incompatibility" so that, in Part II, I can turn my attention to analyzing *A Prague Cemetery* through that lens. Summarizing both parts, ambiguity is that which violates, questions, and challenges to expose the epistemological provisionality of any given narrativizing theory, which is a particular arrangement of the cultural encyclopedia. While that last sentence reads as if ripped from the jargon riddled texts of a continental philosopher, I promise, I define my terms and carefully unpack my argument. But the "Introduction" is a place of signaling, not arguing.

It might be helpful to think of ambiguity as a boiling cauldron filled with churning verbs—violate, question, challenge. Whereas I do not add my definition of "coexistent incompatibility" to the pot, I paint it on the front of the cauldron in capital letters. It is important to remember that coexistent incompatibility is not a binary construction. It's an awareness of the plurality of equiprobable realities that can arise from any given encyclopedia. And before you accuse or dismiss my argument as something akin to naïve relativism, Chapters Two and Three deal with just that issue by tossing Charles S. Peirce's "Firstness" and Umberto Eco's "lines of resistance" into the boiling pot of ambiguity.

In the excursuses, I employ my theory of ambiguity outside the orbit of Echian planets. I show, rather than tell, my argument. And in the last part of *Narrativizing Theories*, I offer up a story, a narrative of my own invention, broken into parts and secreted throughout the text. "The Composer" performs the title, *Narrativizing Theories*. If the arrangement of an encyclopedia is a kind of narrative that is embodied in the world, then *Narrativizing Theories* is the encyclopedia to the arrangement of "The Composer."

3. Francis, *When Art Disrupts Religion*, 140.
4. Francis, *When Art Disrupts Religion*, 141.
5. Francis, *When Art Disrupts Religion*, 141.

This interweaving of text and short story might, perhaps, feel like didacticism, but only because the reader is confronted with the unique opportunity to encounter both encyclopedia and narrative simultaneously, which so rarely happens. The reader is oftentimes solely presented with "The Composer" and then given the difficult task of working backwards to the matter of arrangement. The desire to reverse engineer any given text is, of course, dependent upon the operative hermeneutic, but, in my case, the text/short story entanglement serves to show the way in which a given percept is intimately connected to the encyclopedia that swirls around it. Imagine confronting "The Composer" outside the confines of *Narrativizing Theories* and asking yourself: Could this story have been arranged otherwise than it is? If your answer is, "Yes," then you're well on your way to understanding the role of ambiguity in aesthetics.

While violating, questioning, and challenging sounds a lot like Francis' "disruption," my coexistent incompatibility is both more and less than modern aesthetic theory. First, when I speak of "aesthetics," I do so in such a way that holds its etymology in tension. Aesthetics is art criticism and sense perception or intuition. I'm not saying that art only disrupts, but rather the confrontation with experience itself has the potential to open unforeseen potentialities. These potentialities are value neutral, as judgment can only take place within an already given cultural encyclopedia.

Second, even though my project is theoretical in nature, the world of things is never far. I'm using theory and narrative to understand the fictions that I map onto reality and embody subjunctively—as if they were true—thereby constructing equiprobable worlds that can be held up and compared to other, similar worlds. The question of choice or judgment then is always lurking beneath my argument, like a lidded cauldron waiting to explode. How do I choose between the worldviews constructed from the relationship between the semiotic and material worlds? It's one of my assumptions that aesthetics can play an important role in articulating the choices of any given community, in so far as it uncovers the communal practices and embodied narratives that comprise a community's encyclopedic stew.

Third, I'm most interested in the material aesthetic of S. Brent Plate. And while *Narrativizing Theories* might appear at odds with Plate's work on materiality, it's not—or at least not totally. I, too, am interested in discovering "a religious aesthetic that does not take as its starting and ending point, Beauty, Truth, or God."[6] But rather than focus on only one side of materiality, I am, in this project, exploring the ways in which "beliefs preserve

---

6. Plate, *Walter Benjamin, Religion, and Aesthetics*, viii.

practices as practices preserve beliefs" and how both function "to signify a sufficiently coherent identity to self and other."[7]

Fourth, and finally, it is only fair at the outset that I define religion as a philosophical category and how it connects to narrativizing theories. While much more is said below, religion is, in my thinking, something akin to the theories of implicit religion that define their subject matter as the various conscious or subconscious commitments that I hold and embody in the world. Implicit religion is useful in that it intentionally nudges the secular/sacred balance off kilter and allows me to conceive of religion as something other than that which easily slots into Western, Protestant categories.[8]

One way to view this book is as an analysis of both the commitments that I make in response to ambiguity but also how I navigate the choice between one commitment over another. Pointing towards Part II of this work, my reading of Captain Simone Simonini in *The Prague Cemetery* is simply an analysis of Simonini's commitments that he seeks to map onto the world as if they were true. It is a study of Simonini's implicit religion. I can conceive of nothing more important than connecting ambiguity to implicit religion and then analyzing the embodied commitments that any individual or community makes in the vast and stormy sea of experience.

In the end, as the epigraph suggests, time runs both ways in the fictions that construct an embodied existence. We do make stories out of our lives and live them as if they were true. And though embedded in the concrete world, our narrativizing theories, our stories are in a constant process of emergence. It's not my intention to universalize a theory of ambiguity, however, in a world that defies universalization. In fact, it's the opposite. For even ambiguity is a narrativizing theory that, like all the rest, is provisional.

---

7. Francis, *When Art Disrupts Religion*, 139.
8. Bailey, "Implicit Religion," 271–78.

Part I: A Theory of Ambiguity

1

Slippery Words

You are about to begin reading Italo Calvino's new novel, *If on a winter's night a traveler*. Relax. Concentrate. Dispel every other thought.

—Italo Calvino, *If on a Winter's Night a Traveler*

Introduction

How does one begin a book? It seems easy. Read everything there is to read. Pen an outline. Sit down and allow the muses to flow, watching as, in that moment of inky-black magic, thought transforms into material substance.

The muses, unfortunately, have surrendered their age-old task.

I'm starting at a blank page. Why are opening sentences always so hard? It's the desire to make it zip and zing, catch the reader off guard. I want my first line through sheer, imaginative force to propel her into the cosmos.

The pressure's too great.

What if the opening sentence falls flat, and she closes the book? What if she lays down *Narrativizing Theories* and picks up her smartphone instead?

Beneath this anxiety is a question. How do I usher the reader into an interpretive space that allows her to complete the book she's currently reading? No. Not finish it. That's not what I meant. By "complete," I mean something like bring to fruition, fulfillment, or perfection. I want to pencil the lines and then watch as she fills them with unimaginable colors.

But perhaps this is too much to ask of any first sentence, and I should move on to other, pragmatic necessities. I find that this aimlessness, however, introduces my topic in an irregular and tangential way: to introduce ambiguity, aesthetics, and why I think the two should go together.

Before I begin I need to answer one, niggling question. Why does aesthetics need a theory of ambiguity to inform it? Aesthetics, in my estimation, has been held captive by *the* transcendentals. Not only has it concerned itself with Beauty, Truth, and the Good, but also with the mother of all transcendentals—God. Left to rot in the sun, materiality, sense perception, and embodiment have been eschewed for their more perfect brethren. Aesthetics, in other words, has been traditionally Plotinian over against the πάντα ῥεῖ of Heraclitus or the swerve of Lucretius.

To take in the continuum of sense perceptions and from that to formulate any kind of understanding about the world, I need both a thing and a concept.[1] The thing, object, or percept, should never be taken for granted. While a percept is there, confronting and pushing back on me, I can't know it fully because an object is always and already a semioticized *thing*. Aesthetics needs a theory of ambiguity because the latter reminds the former that I'm neither confined by the object nor the concept. When I confront a percept,[2] there is always the possibility for new openings, categories, and ways of understanding. Neither I nor the percept—nor its category—is fixed.[3]

Ambiguity brings fluidity to aesthetics, like the opening sentence of a book that confronts a reader by establishing itself as that which *is* before asking that same reader to complete the book through a work of interpretation. But an aesthetic of ambiguity doesn't leave the process of understanding there. A confrontation with ambiguity pushes and pulls, grows and stretches—through the work of perception and interpretation—the cultural encyclopedia of the reader and, when at its best, beckons her towards the horizon of the unknown.

On Ambiguity

Ambiguity isn't vagueness. It's *not* the antithesis of clarity. While the *Oxford English Dictionary* lists several definitions,[4] all of which leave something wanting, I'm interested in exploring that which is capable of "being understood in two or more ways." Artificial, perhaps, but I divide

---

1. And the question of which came first, thing or concept, is too tiring and laborious a conversation. We simply do not know. But we need both to make sense of the world and if one needs *a priori* categories to accept that, then so be it.

2. By "percept," I mean, simply, an object of perception.

3. As a brute and physical fact, the percept, obviously, is fixed. I cannot, in other words, by a sheer bending of the mind manipulate the physical compound of a rock. I can, however, change both my understanding of it and its position within my cultural encyclopedia. In doing so, the rock's cultural category is subject to changing, stretching, and slipping between categories. A brute, physical fact, in this way, is not fixed.

4. "ambiguity, n.," *OED Online*, http://www.oed.com.du.idm.oclc.org/viewdictionaryentry/Entry/6144: "wavering of opinion . . . an uncertainty . . . capability of being understood in two or more ways . . . a word or phrase susceptible of more than one meaning."

ambiguity into three distinct but overlapping discourses: literary,[5] philosophic, and scientific.

Literary Ambiguity

When one thinks of ambiguity, one most likely brings to mind literary ambiguity. Immortalized by William Empson, this kind of ambiguity is defined "as an indecision as to what you mean, an intention to mean several things, a probability that one or other or both of two things has been meant, and the fact that a statement has several meanings."[6] Literary ambiguity can be summarized as a lexeme having two or more lexical entries or, as I suggest, a word or cultural artifact capable of being understood in two or more ways. When I come across the word "bank," I am, due to its lexical possibilities, struck by an instance of ambiguity. Does it mean a place where money is exchanged or the place whereupon young lovers meet to ingest an egg salad sandwich?

Ever so close to literary ambiguity is the definition posited by semioticians, who extend ambiguity to that of the *context* of a given lexeme. "A sentence," they write, "is ambiguous when it can be interpreted in two or more different ways."[7] For them, ambiguity is tangled up with both homonymy and polysemy, an entanglement that is the basis for creative language.[8] Why's that? Because literary texts are less constrained in their communicative goals than nonfictional texts.[9] Show, in other words, don't tell. The constraints or communicative effects of nonfiction are directed at clarity, understanding, and brevity, constraints commonly challenged by literature, the latter of which, à la James Joyce, pushes against the conventions of language and culture.

Literary ambiguity addresses the problem of multiple interpretations coexisting at the same time.[10] Similar to the visual arts, the question arises: Who is responsible for generating meaning—the viewer or the creator? Ambiguity, when considering a literary text, foregrounds multiple interpretations and expressions that belongs to two or more categories.[11]

---

5. By literary, I mean, generally speaking, aesthetics, where aesthetics means the academic study of art. This is a broad section in which visual and pictorial art are also represented.
6. Empson, *Seven Types of Ambiguity*, 5.
7. Violi and Steiner, "Ambiguity," 23.
8. Violi and Steiner, "Ambiguity," 23.
9. Winkler, *Ambiguity*, 17.
10. Winkler, *Ambiguity*, 17.
11. Gamboni, *Potential Images*, 13.

Slightly askew from either author or reader, Christoph Bode writes that meaning is generated from the event of literature itself, resulting in an ambiguity defined as the "conspicuous proliferation of multiple meanings."[12] Those that would say a sign or a text in its *literariness*—outside the use of everyday language—is both ambiguous and self-referential commit an error. A sign, at its most general, points to something else.[13] If it must point to something else in order to signify, Bode asks, then how can it also be self-referential?

This calls into question most of literary aesthetics.

A sign that is self-referential is no longer a sign and, hence, can't signify. This is a problem for literary critics that claim *Moby Dick as a text* signifies x and is simultaneously self-referential because it breaks from everyday language and therefore opens new possibilities for the condition of language. Both can't be true.

Rather than seeking a referent or that to which a sign points, Bode's aesthetic of ambiguity searches out events or that which just is.

Bode argues that for a writer to create an event, he or she must break all primary codes.[14]

> The aesthetics of ambiguity offers access to <<meaning as an event>>, to the experience of experience . . . art and a literature which, by striving after auto-referentiality, transcend their former semiotic status and present themselves as free offers of experience met with an aesthetics which, knowing it can never prove conclusively the objectivity of what it talks about, can only submit the same offer: to enter, to expose oneself to an experience and to see what happens.[15]

Bode's event is essential to ambiguity—the nature of experience to call into question cultural categories and concepts while also simultaneously probing the boundaries of reality.

Literary ambiguity, in the end, takes a word, sentence, text, object, or visual artwork and sees it as pointing to multiple meanings in a cultural encyclopedia.[16] To some this object is aesthetic only insofar as it is self-referential, but to others self-referentiality is an undoing of the concept of the sign itself. In these cases, the focus is shifted to the category of event

---

12. Bode, "The Aesthetics of Ambiguity," 73.
13. Eco, "Sign," 936.
14. Bode, "The Aesthetics of Ambiguity," 82.
15. Bode, "The Aesthetics of Ambiguity," 82–3.
16. I will use "cultural encyclopedia" throughout this chapter, but I will not define it until Chapter Two, wherein I turn my full attention to Umberto Eco.

over against the concept of sign. Literary ambiguity is concerned with the coexistence of multiple meanings and the way in which the artifact and the reader work together to establish a possible meaning.

Philosophic Ambiguity

While literary ambiguity overlaps with philosophic ambiguity, it's important to reiterate that my categories of ambiguity are arbitrary, if useful heuristics. They aren't concrete, even though my handprints are permanently set within them. My understanding of literary ambiguity houses both semiotics and the visual arts. My definition of philosophic ambiguity comprises classic, analytic, and speculative philosophy, as well as some good old-fashioned metaphysics.

Both Aristotle and the stoics discussed ambiguity. Where Aristotle defined ambiguity as an instance of an expression or name having more than one meaning,[17] the Stoics, or at least Chrysippus, argued that one person may understand a word in various ways.[18] So far this is little different from literary ambiguity. Things changed, however, when analytic philosophers started to analyze lexical, syntactic, and pragmatic ambiguities. It was important for them to say what ambiguity is not.

Philosophic ambiguity is not polysemy, vagueness, context sensitivity, under-specification and generality, or sense and reference transfer. It is, rather, an instance of two lexical entries corresponding to the same word. But, unfortunately, distinctions abound. There is an elementary ambiguity, which is semantic or lexical in nature.[19] There is an indecisive ambiguity, which is a psychological occurrence that can't decide between two potential meanings a speaker intends.[20] And there is a manifold ambiguity, which is when an expression is used two ways at once, assigning the utterance multiple interpretations.[21] For *Narrativizing Theories*, this summary is meant to be useful in so far as it carves out philosophic ambiguity's unique space, over against literary ambiguity's.

Finally, John D. Caputo defines ambiguity as "the condition that makes meaning possible by making pure and unambiguous meaning impossible."[22]

17. Aristotle, "On Sophistical Refutations," 280–1.
18. Cf. Sennet, 5 and Catherine Atherton, *The Stoics on Ambiguity* (Cambridge: Cambridge University Press, 1993).
19. Scheffler, *Beyond the Letter*, 13.
20. Scheffler, *Beyond the Letter*, 16.
21. Scheffler, *Beyond the Letter*, 17.
22. Caputo, "In Praise of Ambiguity," 20.

Binaries not only found each other but make each other possible. Unreadability, for example, is the condition of possibility for reading.[23] By analogy then, ambiguity is the ground that makes meaning possible. "Clarity and ambiguity," he writes:

> should not be viewed as simple logical opposites on a timeless spectrum but different stages in the process of making meaning, or producing meaning as an effect. Clarity is a late product . . . at the end of the process . . . Ambiguity . . . belongs to an earlier matinal stage, to a deeper stratum of meaning . . . Ambiguity is ambi-valent . . . bristling with multiple values, indeed poly-valent, alive with possibilities that cannot be neatly ordered or contained.[24]

Philosophic ambiguity, in the end, is distinct from literary ambiguity in its focus. Whereas literary ambiguity is concerned with the proliferation of meaning, holding multiple interpretations in tension, and the role of the reader, philosophic ambiguity is by and large analytic in its focus on the systems of language, communication, and Logical Forms. But as Bode ended the former section with a shift away from sign to that of event, Caputo does the same for philosophic ambiguity. For him, ambiguity is the condition of possibility for meaning in its insistence on making unambiguous meaning impossible. Ambiguity is a constant reminder to analytic philosophy that its quest, while admirable, is ultimately quixotic.

Scientific Ambiguity

While so much of science values clarity and precision, which is great when my daughter ingests a dose of amoxicillin, it's not without its ambiguities. Scientific ambiguity springs from the theories of information and chaos and takes on the eerie properties of paradigm-shifting, broken symmetry, and quantum indeterminacy.[25]

To begin with the most general, scientific ambiguity is akin to Thomas Kuhn's "anomaly."[26] Rather than an incremental progression by the accumulation of signs that points to facts in the world, an anomaly will often rise

---

23. Caputo, "In Praise of Ambiguity," 22.

24. Caputo, "In Praise of Ambiguity," 25.

25. Though a full analysis of ambiguity and information theory will have to wait until the following chapter wherein I discuss information theory's influence over Eco's theory of ambiguity.

26. Cf. Kuhn, *The Structure of Scientific Revolutions* and Hoffmann, *The Same and Not the Same*. The latter is a study of ambiguity from the perspective of chemistry.

that contradicts the prevailing paradigm. When an anomaly can no longer be ignored, scientists are forced to grapple with it, test it, and ultimately account for it. This leads to a scientific revolution or to a new, unforeseen possibility in the description of reality. Anomaly is a scientific ambiguity—it is that which calls into question the traditional codes.

Another way to think about scientific ambiguity is through the concept of oscillation in sense perception. Confronted with a constant stimulus, pattern perception fluctuates between two or more possible interpretations. This plurality of interpretation is often referred to as "multistability."[27]

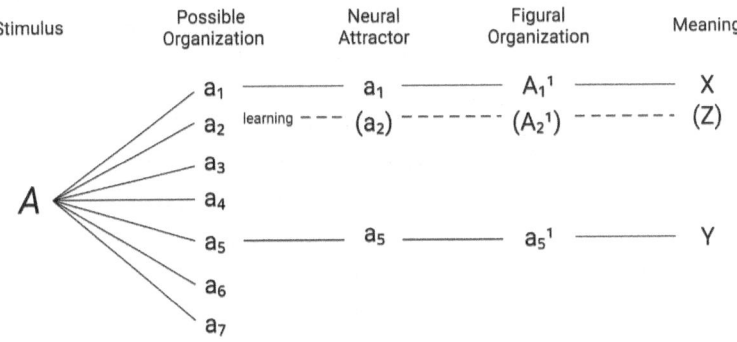

Looking at figure 1,[28] ambiguity is best represented by the six "possible organizations" that correspond to "A," the one, concrete stimulus. Notice, too, that how I organize a sense perception is separate from that sense perception's meaning and that three different meanings are possible given six possible organizational schemes. The possible organization of "a_2" represents an organizational schema that is not given, automated, or spontaneous. It has, in other words, no entry in the cultural encyclopedia and must, therefore, be learned, which leads to the possible generation of new meanings.

Scientific ambiguity can also mean "the coexistence or confluence of two or more incompatible aspects in the same reality."[29] While this, at first glance, seems paradoxical, it's the result of having to rethink science and human perceptions in the wake of the quantum revolution. With discoveries in science (Albert Einstein, Werner Karl Heisenberg, etc.), philosophers began to focus on the "dynamics of the processes of transformation

---

27. Kruse and Stadler, "The Function of Meaning in Cognitive Order Formation," 5.
28. Kruse and Stadler, "The Function of Meaning in Cognitive Order Formation," 10.
29. Caglioti, "Ambiguity," 53.

rather than on Aristotle's statics of the objects."[30] "In conclusion," one commentator writes:

> complex concepts of quantum physics and the structure of matter are intimately connected with optical illusions, paradoxes, and ambiguities, features usually attributed to the world of art rather than to science. Both art and science are produced, emotionally and rationally, by our thinking. And our thinking proceeds chaotically, on the jagged watershed of a permanent cultural value: ambiguity.[31]

Scientific ambiguity, when "taken as bivalency," is the "simultaneous presence of two aspects of reality that are incompatible with each other."[32] Rather jarring to the mind, the reader is well within her rights to ask the question: How can reality have two simultaneous presences (cf. fig. 2)?

The point is that ambiguity shows up in the sciences as well as in the humanities, and that scientific ambiguity bleeds into literary theory via Eco's information theory. When Eco, who I will continually be analyzing throughout *Narrativizing Theories*, describes ambiguity as that which "must be defined as a mode of violating the rules of the code"[33] or as an important device that functions as an introduction to the aesthetic experience,[34] he is not elucidating literary, semiotic, or philosophic ambiguity. He is, rather, drawing on a scientific ambiguity rooted in information theory[35] and bringing it to bear on aesthetics, an aesthetics understood as a discourse on art and literature but not wholly divorced from sense perception. I am, however, getting ahead myself.

Scientific ambiguity can also be defined as the breaking of symmetry (where symmetry is defined as invariance under transformation), the "coexistence, at a critical point, of two aspects or schemes of reality which are mutually exclusive and which have become physically observable"[36] or "as the coevolution or coexistence of two mutually incompatible aspects of a same reality inside a single structure."[37] Imagine turning an empty wine bottle in your hands, labels removed, and being unable to perceive any change

---

30. Gleick, *Time Travel: A History*, 54.
31. Gleick, *Time Travel: A History*, 55.
32. Fenoglio, "Preface to the Italian Edition," xv. Cf. Caglioti, "Perception of Ambiguous Figures," 463–78.
33. Eco, *A Theory of Semiotics*, 263.
34. Eco, *A Theory of Semiotics*, 274.
35. Again, I will show this in the following chapters.
36. Caglioti, *The Dynamics*, 17. Cf. Caglioti, "Perception of," 464.
37. Caglioti, "Perception of," 477.

in the structure even though the bottle is changing over time. That's symmetry. When it's broken, because of, let's say, a bubble or streak in the glass, your perception of the bottle will alter. The reality of the bottle spinning or changing over time will be made visible.

Perception is a dynamic instability, implying a scientific ambiguity, an intersection between natural structures and humanity's cultural relationship with them.[38]

> At the level of conceptual synthesis, a structure appears qualitatively symmetrical until the moment in which, following a scansion of the structure itself, a dynamic instability of the perceptive process is produced: and one realizes that he has extracted information, or given a new meaning, or has been enlightened by an idea.[39]

This is true in science, art, music, and even those funny pictures that oscillate between a duck and a bunny. In scientific ambiguity, a human mind decides what to see when confronted with a given percept.

Ambiguity's Conclusion

In her introductory essay on the state of ambiguity across disciplines, Susanne Winkler suggests that the governing question of modern ambiguity theory is the question of where ambiguity occurs—in the production or perception of a percept?[40] Following from this is another, though connected, question: Is ambiguity—produced or perceived—strategic or nonstrategic? For Winkler and others, this results in four potentialities: 1) strategic production, 2) nonstrategic production, 3) strategic perception, and 4) nonstrategic perception.[41] All four potentialities are present in both literary and philosophic ambiguity, but perhaps not scientific, where scientists set out to analyze and understand nonstrategic perceptual ambiguity.

Most interesting, for me, is the strategic production of ambiguity in literary texts. Why? "Strategic production of ambiguity," Winkler writes:

> is a central issue in literary criticism and rhetoric . . . While the premise that ambiguity is employed strategically in literary texts can be deemed valid, it is often difficult to identify its effects.

---

38. Caglioti, *The Dynamics*, 12.
39. Caglioti, *The Dynamics*, 110.
40. Winkler, *Ambiguity*, 17.
41. Winkler, *Ambiguity*, 18.

It is precisely for this reason that literary texts lend themselves extremely well to examining the functions of ambiguity.[42]

In *Narrativizing Theories*, I am concerned with literary ambiguity: the proliferation of meaning, holding multiple interpretations in tension, and the role of the reader. I am not interested in any literary ambiguity, however, but that which is best depicted by Eco, whose literary ambiguity is grounded in the perceptual sciences. Without saying too much here, Eco's ambiguity takes the polysemy of aesthetics seriously. It's an ambiguity that stresses both the creative construction of meaning and the hard perception of the senses. And in a strange twist, it also takes into consideration Caputo's foundational ambiguity, which is seen in Eco's use of Charles Sanders Peirce.

By ambiguity, to fully define my term, I mean the coexistence of two or more incompatible aspects of the same reality. This coexistent incompatibility is what I bring into conversation with Eco's aesthetics and Plate's material aesthetic. Ambiguity taken as a coexistent incompatibility can arise from any percept, whether that percept is a thing or a cultural artifact. Given my emphasis on a literary ambiguity informed by its scientific sibling, it's no surprise that most of *Narrativizing Theories* focuses on literary analyses and the strategic production of ambiguity.

The Composer: Part I
The Meeting between Ed Abernathy and his Editor, Gina

"Are you familiar with the Voynich manuscript?"

"No. Should I be?" I sat back, searching my memory.

"The Atlantic ran a story on it—a fifteenth-century manuscript written in gibberish. No one was able to interpret it though. It's meaningless."

"And?"

"They claimed that someone cracked it. Figured it out. Some old lady's," Gina glanced at her MacBook, "herbiary."

"Herbiary?"

"Like bestiary, but with plants."

"Bestiary? Look, I—"

"Spare me your jokes. Point is that *The Atlantic* had over two-hundred thousand clicks. We need that kind of traffic."

"You want me to write a story on Voynich?"

"No, not that. It's been done. We need another angle." Gina ran a hand through her thin hair. "A De Vinci Code kind of story."

---

42. Winkler, *Ambiguity*, 18.

"What do you have in mind?"

She turned her rose-gold computer to face me. "This."

"C'mon. That's legend. It never happened."

"Couldn't care less. That's not the point. Clicks are. You write it, they'll click. Get out there, dig around. Find someone who was there."

"They're all dead."

"Then a daughter or a granddaughter of someone who was. I don't really care. I just want a copy on my desk by the fourteenth."

"Three weeks?" I tilted back my chair to look at the tiled ceiling. I was in a prison of dunces. "Who's paying for this?"

"Whatever you need. Just ask. This is serious. Patrick wants to see it, too."

"Why the hell does corporate care if *The Atlantic* beats us on clicks? They always beat us."

"That's the wrong question. In fact, questions are meaningless when it comes to Patrick. Just get it done."

"Why not Paguyo or Martinez? Both know music better than I do."

"That's the point. Patrick wants someone to write it who can communicate it to the masses without all the jargon. Don't use 'tonic' or 'allegro' or even 'measure.' Write it so I can understand it, and maybe even enjoy it."

"You hate music."

"Exactly."

I left Gina's office and caught the "Q." I exited three blocks from the public library.

Walking always cleared my mind. The white noise. The anonymity. The sheer movement of city streets. I was part of a process from which I couldn't extricate myself.

There's a word. "Extricate." Couldn't use that in my story. Or "from which." Ending with prepositions is fine now. Why? Because people need simplicity, and journalists need a third-grade intellect. It's our screens and our all-consuming Google.

Once upon a time.

That's how I should begin my story, since this whole thing's a fairytale anyway. Like Atari's *E.T.* or UPN's *South Beach*, a story like this could ruin my career.

I turned the corner and saw the pillared building. It loomed overhead, stern and imposing. The marble steps, leading upwards, implied an ordered reality, an eye in the middle of life's storm. As much as I loved this place, desired it even, it frightened me.

"Classical music?"

The librarian looked up. "Yes?"

"I'm looking for anything you have on the composer, Zuravel Ostrava Martynov."

His fingers blazed over the keyboard, clicking and clacking.

"Floor three. Section seven. Would you like me to show you?"

"No. I can find it."

Thick stacks ran endlessly beneath the vaulted ceiling. I could smell the bindings. Feel the ink. The vertigo of knowledge hit me like a backhanded slap.

I always left the library with three or more novels. Books I wanted to read, but for which I couldn't find the time. Maybe Saturday.

Didn't Gaiman just release a new one? Now there was a storyteller. I wonder what he would do with Martynov?

Here it was.

The book that Gina had told me about, *The Composer: A Symbol Burnt in St. Petersburg* by Nikolayevich Romanov Diletsky.

On Religious Aesthetics

Aesthetics is a strange category rife with slippage. Its use is often indeterminate, idiosyncratic, and disparate.[43] While it did not begin properly as an academic field until 1750 when Alexander Gottlieb Baumgarten coined the term "aesthetics" from the Greek *aisthesis* (perception by the senses), aesthetics has a much older lineage wherein the Greek τεχνή (craft, skill, or technical trade), ποίησις (making, creation, or the poetic arts), and τὸ καλόν (beautiful, useful, or good) are all jumbled together in a grab-bag of curios and miscellany.

Aesthetics, on the one hand, is concerned with that which is beautiful—or Beautiful—and therefore with the fine arts or, when capitalized, with theology. That is, until recently, when aesthetes turned their attention towards culture, pop or otherwise. On the other hand, aesthetics is interested in perception, cognition, and knowledge. It questions how one might come to know reality through the continuum of the senses, while problematizing the role of language, categories, and culture in understanding the world. But it also has a long and august theological and religious tradition that considers the role that the senses play in divine revelation, as well as, more recently, the materiality of religious practices.

With these possible meanings and launching points, it is the burden of any philosopher to describe what she means when using the word "aesthetics." That is my purpose in this section wherein I not only carve out my

---

43. Eagleton, *The Ideology of the Aesthetic*, 3.

usage from the muddled history of the term, but also begin to describe what an aesthetics of ambiguity might look like. I focus mostly on religious aesthetics and its trajectory towards materiality, but also on the way in which my understanding of ambiguity as a coexistent incompatibility confronts religious aesthetics.

Transcendental Aesthetics

A transcendental aesthetic engages the categories of the Beautiful, the True, and the Good (not to mention God) and considers how these transcendentals illuminate divine revelation. While this field of discourse has a long history, of which Eco is a part (though, it must be said, from a nonconfessional standpoint), it has been most recently dominated by Hans Urs von Balthasar. It is nearly impossible to summarize the voluminous writings of von Balthasar. While I have neither the time nor inclination to do so, it's important to get a sense of what von Balthasar is up to. I must stress that I grapple with von Balthasar, ever so briefly, not to understand him better, but to understand what *I* mean by aesthetics.

Von Balthasar's basic aim is to treat beauty (*pulchrum*) as the way God's goodness (*bonum*) "gives itself and is expressed by God and understood by man as the truth (*verum*)."[44] What is key is that von Balthasar sets out to distinguish between an aesthetic theology and a theological aesthetics. The former tries to comprehend the experience of divine beauty by means of some preconceived notion of the beautiful and thus corrupts biblical values and limits Christian perception. The latter beholds the unique beauty of a revelatory form as something freely given by God.

Von Balthasar seeks to account for the "subjective evidence" of revelation, considering how the beautiful form(s) of the divine are beheld by the faithful, before turning to the "objective" basis for such experiences of revelatory beauty, which is absolutely and inescapably God's Incarnation in Christ—a reality that von Balthasar regards as the foundation of any possible Christian theological aesthetics.

If I can put it bluntly, von Balthasar takes the two-thousand-year history of aesthetics and rethinks it through the "injected narrative" of Jesus' incarnation or *forma Christi*.[45] By positing this as a starting or initial point, von Balthasar is able to order his cosmos in such a way that he can arrive at

---

44. Von Balthasar, *The Glory of the Lord*, 13 and 151.

45. Peters, *Sigurd's Lament*, 53–55 and 206–8, for what I mean by an "injected narrative." See also, Lawson, "Cognition," 83, and Seligman, *Ritual and Its Consequences*, 25, for a similar phenomenon known in ritual theory as the "initial point."

a properly understood aesthetic (in the sense of both perception and art). But, as Paul Crowther has shown, much of von Balthasar's logic, even when read generously, falls flat.[46] Perhaps another way to examine von Balthasar regarding *Narrativizing Theories* is to suggest that his aesthetic seeks to do away with any coexistent incompatibilities in the Christian worldview. Von Balthasar's univocal aesthetic is extremely low in ambiguity.

Helpful is the definition of Christian transcendence that one of von Balthasar's main commentators provides:

> Christian transcendence is the encounter of the human person with God in the world, an encounter in which the empirical facticity of the external world is sacralized in light of God's creative activity, and in which those subjective human limitations that can be ascribed to egoism are healed by a grace whose ever-receding horizon makes any exhaustive understanding of salvific transcendence impossible to attain.[47]

This kind of transcendence can be understood as a human's encounter with God in the world. It focuses on the ways in which Beauty enraptures a human as she beholds an object, a transcendental aesthetic that focuses on Beauty, Truth, and the Good in so far as they reveal the form, from within themselves, of the divine, which is the *forma Christi* or the illumined humanity and divinity of Jesus.

While von Balthasar has constructed a house that most transcendental aesthetes cannot escape, very few engage von Balthasar without eventually remodeling. One example of this is Christopher D. Denny's critical extension of von Balthasar. To Denny, one does not just behold a percept and through it that to which it points, but rather participates with the percept (much like Bode's event). It is in that participation or performance that the form is not only revealed but also appropriated for any given community[48]—likewise, Frank Burch Brown, Alejandro García-River, and Jeremy Begbie, all of whom, in some way, build upon, critique, and extend that which von Balthasar has done.

In most cases, the operative transcendental aesthetic seeks to place the transcendental—Beauty, Truth, God—into conversation with culture, power, or identity. Brown's "neo-aesthetics" exemplifies this approach, "which is distinguished by the attempt to take seriously such complex aesthetic

---

46. Crowther, *How Pictures Complete Us*, 159–160. See also, Kilby, *Balthasar*, 167.
47. Denny, *A Generous Symphony*, 8.
48. Denny, 275.

responses and judgments and to recognize the extent to which they are an ingredient in all of culture, and not least in religion."[49]

In an interesting move, Brown takes a transcendental aesthetic and, placing it in conversation with culture, argues that there is no pure aesthetic object and therefore nothing outside of the gaze of a religious philosopher. In fact, he argues, many artists—though materialists—seek to account for the "unknowable more" of experience. Looked at this way, a transcendental aesthetic focuses neither on religion nor art, but rather an integration of the two that has the power to formulate a theological ethic.

Whether of the von Balthasarian type or the more culturally oriented approaches of Denny, Brown, and García-Rivera, a transcendental aesthetic is preeminently concerned with either how God illuminates experience or how experience engages, appropriates, or symbiotically relates to God. A transcendental aesthetic, in other words, is theologically driven and rarely, if ever, operates outside the "reality" of God. This raises the question: Is the very idea of God antithetical to a theory of ambiguity understood as coexistent incompatibility? Or could someone like Brown argue that all ambiguities resolve in a Christian conceptualization of God even if not all are accounted for in a theological ethic? If God implies a univocalization of reality, then how does one account for a plurivocality in perception, particularly regarding incompatible perceptions that are coexistent?

Gesa Elsbeth Thiesen summarizes this approach well.

> Beauty is not an extra, it is essential to all existence. Truth or goodness without becomes dull, lifeless, boring, formalistic and cold. It is beauty . . . which excites and nourishes human feeling, desire, thought and imagination. It is the splendour of beauty that makes the true and the good whole. The magnitude of beauty in nature and in all human creation, wherever it is experienced, gives us a glimpse of the beauty of God, therein lies its saving power. In this way beauty becomes a way to God and a manifestation of God at the same time. God's beauty is what draws us to God.[50]

I am not interested in a transcendental aesthetic. To be clear: Whenever I refer to a religious aesthetics, I do not mean a transcendental aesthetic or an aesthetic that, starting from God, desires to illuminate experience via Beauty. I also don't mean an aesthetic that seeks to explore a perceived fundamental Beauty and its entanglement with creation. If there is a critical unawareness in a transcendental aesthetic, then it's in the thoroughly

---

49. Brown, *Religious Aesthetics*, 13.
50. Thiessen, ed. *Theological Aesthetics*, 6.

western assumption (rooted in τὸ καλόν) that the beautiful and the good are somehow intertwined or entangled.

My starting point is wholly different in that it asks the question: Could one imagine an aesthetic that accounts for both sense perception and art that is not caught in the transcendental traps of beauty and goodness equaling a neo-Platonic unity, oneness, or God?

Material Aesthetics

Philosophical aesthetics (via Baumgarten and Immanuel Kant) first asked the question of how materiality, sense perception, and the body related to the supersensible, reason, and logic. This approach was largely forgotten when Georg Wilhelm Friedrich Hegel transformed aesthetics into a discourse on the fine arts. Terry Eagleton, among others, sought to restore the foundation of aesthetics as sense perception and hold that in tension with aesthetics as the philosophy of art. Plate, taking his cue from Eagleton, confronted the strange history of aesthetics and argued that a religious—as opposed to theological—aesthetic should account for both materiality and semiotics, for both experience and idea.

A material aesthetic is concerned with what Plate calls the "skinscape" or that liminal space between *aesthetica naturalis* and *aesthetica artificialis*.[51] Plate, going back to his dissertation, conceives of an aesthetic that doesn't rely on transcendence and representation. His key concerns are the way the "body perceives the words and images of the world, and the way these bodily perceptions interact with other human bodies."[52] He accomplishes

---

51. "Aesthetics" can be defined in two ways: one, aesthetics is sensory perception (things perceived) and is distinct from conceptual knowledge (things known). Two, aesthetics is the philosophical study of style, art, beauty, and taste. The former is considered to be *aesthetica naturalis*, while the latter is considered to be *aesthetica artificialis*. By "religious aesthetics," I am relying on Plate's definition and understanding of how religion and aesthetics are mutually informing. In one sense, aesthetics focuses on how we perceive and create our worlds through sense perception, which is then responsible for the formation of community and society. Here Plate sees the dialectic between *naturalis* and *artificialis*—between embodiment and objects/arts—as forming an originary point for the study of religion. How? Because "fundamental to this," Plate writes, "is the contention that sense perception is a central point of mediation for the reception, creation, and reproduction of social-sacred space." A religious aesthetics then is that which focuses on the liminal space between the dialectic of *naturalis* and *artificialis* and, from that vantage point, analyzes religious worlds. Likewise, by an "invented religious aesthetics," Plate means that which is informed by Walter Benjamin's anti-beauty aesthetic that focuses on fragments and interconnection over transcendentals and individual contemplation. Cf. Plate, "The Skin of Religion," 167–8.

52. Plate, *Inventing*, 1.

this shift away from transcendental aesthetics and towards material aesthetics by closely examining Walter Benjamin's insistence that aesthetics should concern itself with communal dispersal (the theater) rather than the disembodied consciousness of a single individual (the novel). Materialist in orientation, Plate writes of Benjamin:

> Once in the realm of the corporeal, the emphasis on the aesthetics of the single individual is shifted outward to the aesthetic interaction in and between others. Among these 'other' interactions are the interactions between word and images, between bodies and technology, between words and technology, or between others.[53]

This move towards materiality and the body is necessarily away from the beauty and goodness of τὸ καλόν. Instead of beauty, there is only fragment. Instead of the neo-Platonic good, there is only movement (like that of Lucretius).

Plate begins by calling his material aesthetic, "an invented religious aesthetic,"[54] which emphasizes interconnection beyond the individual, logocentric self. Aesthetics, in Plate's reading of Benjamin, is about taking the world apart, rummaging through its ruins, and putting it back together in creative ways.[55] This is an allegorical model (as opposed to symbolic) and viewed as a "process of demythologizing and remythologizing without a final stable order."[56]

The shift away from Beauty, Truth, or God—a transcendental aesthetic—is towards a materiality, which leaves open the possibility for that which is "mystical."[57] Plate's aesthetic is not an *arche*. It is only one fertile field among many that,[58] grounded in aesthetic experience, highlights the dialectic between material culture and human creative activities.[59] The site of Plate's dialectic is what he calls "the skinscape," a place wherein natural aesthetics can examine cognitions and perceptions, while artificial aesthetics can explore mediums and messages. "The skinscape," he writes, "stands at the crux of the matter . . . it happens at in-between, mediated places. From

---

53. Plate, *Inventing*, 1.
54. Plate, *Inventing*, 1.
55. Plate, *Inventing*, 1.
56. Plate, *Walter Benjamin*, 79.
57. Dunn, "What Really Happened," 881–902.
58. Cf. Roberts, *Encountering Religion*, 3.
59. Cf. Roberts, *Encountering Religion*, 3.

this focal point, it unfolds outward to become the foundation stone in the construction of social-sacred space."[60]

Where there is overlap between Plate's position and mine is in considering the skinscape as an instantiation of ambiguity. Plate's aesthetic both highlights and accounts for plurivocality—in distinction to von Balthasar's univocality—in sense perception and meaning making. In many ways, it's an aesthetic that recognizes coexistent incompatibility, though by utilizing a different bibliography. The main difference between Plate's skinscape and my understanding of ambiguity is that coexistent incompatibilities show how Plate's skinscape both arises and functions, while also going one step further in seeking to account for potentialities and the creation of new knowledge.

This leads me to the question: What does a material aesthetic achieve or do that a transcendental aesthetic does not? First, I think, it seeks to do away with or at least account for injected narratives or what I have called univocalities. It acknowledges that while I have starting points when considering the construction of reality via sense perception, I can, at the very least, work from the ground up.

Second, it maintains that this ground-up approach is inextricably linked to the semiotic world. Once sense perception is received or the continuum partitioned, it nearly instantaneously enters a semiotic or cultural world. A material aesthetic acknowledges this and seeks to maintain a balance between the material and the semiotic. A transcendental aesthetic, however, often takes the material as contentless, meaningless, or empty in that it only points to the truer reality that is revealed through form.[61] A material aesthetic is neither fully sense perception nor imaginative creativity (cultural semiosis). It is somewhere in between, accounting for both, while—and this is where coexistent incompatibility is at work—suggesting new possibilities.

Religious Aesthetics

You will have noticed, no doubt, that I have yet to define the religion in my *religious* aesthetic. And though tedious, defining what I mean by religion is a necessary task.

---

60. Plate, *Skinscape*, 173.

61. Though, as I have shown via Brown, some transcendental religious aesthetes have set out to correct this.

I've previously suggested three definitions that I take into consideration regarding religion. One:[62]

> Religion is a cultural system or process stemming from the encyclopedia of any particular culture or language that, in turn, is negotiated or embodied in the world—an encyclopedia constructing and shaping a reality,[63] a reality formulating and informing an encyclopedia.[64] Religion is that narrative—wrested from the relationship between a culture's encyclopedia and reality—by which any community orders and makes sense of its world. It is that subjunctive, 'as if' reality that any particular community posits and embodies.[65] This understanding of religion is not meant to be a universal definition that transcends culture and language, but rather an emic category negotiated by any particular culture and language and that, within any framework, is both absolute and absolutely fluid.[66]

Two, I see religion similarly to theorists of implicit religion where religion is seen as one or more "commitment(s)" that intentionally nudge the secular/sacred balance off kilter.[67] Three, I am also highly influenced by Mary Dunn's radical empiricism, which seeks to account for the "unknowable more" that juxtaposes a multiplicity of narratives in the hopes of engineering an encounter between the scholar's world and that of her subject's.[68]

The tension between the material and semiotic world is maintained in my understanding of religion, which is *as if* in that it's an invented semiotic that's typically embodied or celebrated in community. Narratives are meaningless unless they are acted upon and lived in the sensible world. But every culture is free to do what it will with the category of religion. I'm only defining what *I mean* by religion. It's not my goal to sound either harsh or dismissive, but words are only useful in so far as they're used in relation

---

62. Peters, "Reading Religion," 2.

63. In what is becoming an endless introductory chapter on definitions, I should, no doubt, define what I mean by "reality." I will, however, defer to Eco and his explorations into both "lines of resistance" and "common sense." Eco, *Kant and the Platypus*, 54 and 133.

64. Eco, *A Theory of Semiotics*, 66–80 and *Semiotics and the Philosophy of Language*, 46–86. See also, Paolo Desogus, "The Encyclopedia in Umberto Eco's Semiotics," 506–8.

65. Cf. Seligman, *Ritual and Its Consequences*, 25.

66. Fish, "Is There a Text in This Class?," 38–54.

67. Peters, "Telescope + Mirror = Reflections on the Cosmos," 345. Cf. Bailey, "Implicit Religion," 271–78.

68. Peters, "Telescope + Mirror," 345–6 and Mary Dunn, "What Really Happened," 881–902.

to cultural units. My definition or understanding of religion is just that, a way to unpack my cultural units as they exist in my cultural encyclopedia, circumscribed by a million, flittering interpretants.

By religious aesthetics then, I mean, first, an aesthetic that distends into both everyday experience and the inventive accounts of life that humans manufacture to make meaning. This is an aesthetic that considers both sense perception and the poetic (ποιήσις) arts. By religion, I mean something like the celebration (both semiotic and embodied) of a communal narrative that is committedly lived in the subjunctive. And, slamming the two together, religious aesthetics is an approach to aesthetic theory that seeks to account for the *meaning making processes*—the commitments and narratives—of humans, grounded in the everyday, and that takes into consideration the unknowable more of experience. My version of religious aesthetics is never a last word, but rather a provisional exploration into the meanings that humans create.

Conclusion: An Ambiguous Aesthetic

Narrativizing Theories, in many ways, is founded upon the question: How does ambiguity, defined as coexistent incompatibility, change the shape of aesthetics? To me, an aesthetic rooted in ambiguity emphasizes seven propositions.

1. Knowledge, the "fact" that emerges from the relationship between perception and the semiosphere, is provisional.

2. Reality, based on the first proposition, is a kind of narrativization or story that humans tell themselves to live and embody *as if* it were true.

3. Ambiguity implies that all human commitments are ultimately perspectival, equal centers in an infinity of meaning. This is true on micro or local levels and is generalized the further one travels into the expanse of the semiosphere. When localizations and their perspectives clash, then negotiations must ensue. But as far as ambiguity is concerned, there is no deferral to a set of rules established outside of human experience.

4. Ambiguity emphasizes the need for semiotics and materiality in aesthetics. While the starting point of an aesthetics of ambiguity is often a percept, it never eschews the cultural encyclopedia or that which makes meaning possible.

5. Ambiguity defined as coexistent incompatibility stresses that the structures facilitating meaning are iterative and fluid—always expanding and contracting.

6. An aesthetics of ambiguity reveals, when it comes to meaning, that neither the cultural encyclopedia nor the percept is fixed. Both cultural knowledge and the ways in which I understand reality can grow, morph, and radically change.

7. Ambiguity asks humans to pause before viewing the double slits and remain in the discomfort of not knowing, and then, when all the light has passed, to consider the other, incompatible reality.

2

Echoes of Ambiguity

The talking fresco was just a delusion and Ern had gone round the bend like his old man. Or, on the other hand, he was still sane and this uncanny intervention was a real event, was genuinely taking place there in the dangling loft about St. Paul's, there in Ern's world, there in his life. Neither of these alternatives was bearable.

—Alan Moore, *Jerusalem*

Introduction

Umberto Eco has said many things about ambiguity. It is that which "must be defined as a mode of violating the rules of the code."[1] It is an introduction to the aesthetic experience that focuses attention and urges interpretation. It produces further knowledge because it "compels one to reconsider the usual codes and their possibilities."[2] And finally, it is the work of the artist who: "always tries to call our perceptual schemata into question, if in no other way than by inviting us to recognize that in certain circumstances things could also appear to us differently."[3]

Lists of quotes hardly make for compelling argumentation. Would that it were so! This would be a much shorter book. But to step on the next wrung in the ladder that is my argument, I need to contextualize Eco's statements on ambiguity before connecting them with my own ideas about coexistent incompatibilities. This is useful for a few reasons.

One, it puts Eco in conversation with the other theorists of ambiguity as outlined in Chapter One. Two, it details why I think Eco's ambiguity is best suited to engage with my understanding of aesthetics. And three, it

---

1. Eco, *A Theory of Semiotics*, 263.
2. Eco, *A Theory of Semiotics*, 274.
3. Eco, *Kant and the Platypus*, 223.

provides me a foundation upon which I can analyze Eco's use of ambiguity in both his theoretical and creative works. I must stress, however, that this chapter is not seeking to crystalize the career of Eco—semiotician, novelist, and literary critic. For that, you need look elsewhere.[4] This chapter, rather, seeks to contextualize Eco's ambiguity so that I can better wield it within a cross-disciplinary discourse.

Information Theory and Aesthetics

Any time a scholar of the humanities reaches into the sciences and pulls out a convenient metaphor or analogy, you should be wary. I am. Why? Because there is no way that I can understand the ins-and-outs of another, highly specialized, scientific or mathematical discourse. It is enough for me to toil in the fields of texts, let alone the abstract worlds of probability, attractors, or bits. And yet, the revolutions in quantum mechanics, chaos, and information cannot be overstressed for our time. They were and are transformations of the modern social imaginary. We engage the world, think, and construct reality differently because of these monumental scientific paradigm shifts.

"Well," you might say, "it's not enough to understand the implications of a scientific outcome—the philosophy of it, so to speak—without grasping its underlying mathematics."

And, as Glaucon might reply, "That's certainly true!"

"Yes, one has to get the science right to extract meaningful observation from it."

"It is as you say."

"Yes, in our day and age," you ruminate to your wide eyed interlocutor, "the sciences and humanities are not mutually informing."

Eco feels the burden of this line of reasoning. "Some people will object," he writes, "that there can be no effective connections between aesthetics and information theory, and that to draw parallels between the two fields can only be a gratuitous, futile exercise. Possibly so."[5] His solution to this conundrum is to spend the next twenty or so pages proving that he fully understands information theory and its consequences—an honorable labor.

I am in a different position, however. I do not need to examine either the workings of information theory or its current scholarship. Rather, I need to reflect on Eco's version of information theory and how he employed it regarding aesthetics. For it is there that I will find the roots of his theory of

---

4. Caesar, *Umberto Eco*; Radford, *On Eco*; Capozzi, *Reading Eco*; Bondanella, *New Essays on Umberto Eco*.

5. Eco, *The Open Work*, 44.

ambiguity. And so, by way of qualification, if you are either Claude Shannon or Norbert Wiener raised from the dead, I apologize in advance.

To Eco, information theory "calculates the quantity of information contained in a particular message."[6] This can be summarized in a word: surprise. If I am told on August 4th that it will *not* snow, then I am being given a message with very low information. If, on the other hand, Channel 9 News tells me that it will snow tomorrow despite my past experiences, then, "given the improbability of the event," the information contained within the message is extremely high.[7] Information, according to Eco, is an additive quantity, "something added to what one already knows as if it were an original acquisition."[8] This fact, seemingly inconsequential, plays large in Eco's aesthetics of ambiguity.

Eco's information is a measure of "the levels of order and disorder in the organization of a given message."[9] Acts of communication are an organized system governed by fixed laws of probability—a code—and are often disturbed from within or without by disorder, which Eco often refers to as "dis-order," and is only possible given a previously established order (even if only an order of probability). If this is all a bit confusing, imagine it in relation to the rules of English grammar. The alphabet, along with its grammatical laws, serves as a probabilistic order or code by which any message can be communicated. To write, "TRLTSEE" or "TT/RLS/EE," is to convey nothing, because the given letters and symbols are not organized utilizing the code of a shared alphabet. In order to transmit a message, I must first organize my communication according to a set of agreed upon probabilistic codes. I could write, "LETTERS" utilizing the same grouping of letters but within the framework of our agreed upon code, the latter serving two purposes: redundancy and restriction. Given a set of consonants (LTTRS), you could rely on the code's redundancy to make an educated guess at the corresponding vowels needed to complete the message. Second, as I have already alluded to, there is only so much that I can do within a given code in order to convey an intelligible message. The code, in other words, restricts or limits the possibility of intelligible messages that I can send.

The code's order creates predictability and grounds understanding between sender and receiver in a given message. But the more predictable a message, the less *information* it conveys. As counterintuitive as it sounds, TRLTSEE is richer in information than LETTERS. Why? Because the

---

6. Eco, *The Open Work*, 45.
7. Eco, *The Open Work*, 45.
8. Eco, *The Open Work*, 45.
9. Eco, *The Open Work*, 49.

former is jampacked with surprise when encountered against the backdrop of our established and agreed upon code of probability, which in this case is the English alphabet.

To account for "information as surprise," however, you must separate information from meaning. "Monday follows Sunday" is both clear and direct in meaning but doesn't tell you anything new. It's a statement high in meaning but low in information (and remember, information is additive, it must add to something that you already know). Meaning and information, in this way, are related. On one side, meaning requires order and probability. On the other, information needs disorder and entropy. Like Caglioti's symmetry, Eco's informational ambiguity sits at the middle point between the competing factors of a message: order, probability, disorder, and entropy. A probabilistic order allows for communication that is predictable, intelligible, and understandable, but information requires a certain amount of entropy and dis-order. Quoting Norbert Wiener, Eco writes:

> 'A piece of information, in order to contribute to the general information of a community, must say something substantially different from the community's previous common stock of information' . . . [for example] great artists, whose chief merit is that they introduce new ways of saying or doing into their community.[10]

Wiener's comment is the hinge between information theory and the aesthetics of ambiguity. An aesthetic message—like a poem or novel—is the result of the "deliberate 'dis-ordering' of the code . . . precisely in order to violate that system of laws and determinations which make up the code."[11] When encountering an aesthetic message, you are confronting a transmission that deliberately violates or questions "the very order—order *as system of probability*—to which it refers."[12] A poetic message allows for equiprobability in meaning, which forces interpretation and fosters communal negotiation.

As an example of this, consider W. Scott Howard's "Ember Amen," a poetic text that intentionally calls into question the probabilistic code of the English language, while simultaneously reminding its readers that all languages are codes.[13] The effect is heightened by the juxtaposition of

---

10. Eco, *The Open Work*, 53.
11. Eco, *The Open Work*, 66.
12. Eco, *The Open Work*, 66.
13. Howard, "Ember Amen," 14–15. For the full effect of the poem, I have included a copy of the poem and its opposite page, cf. figure 2.1. "Ember Amen" by W. Scott Howard is reprinted from SPINNAKERS (Boulder: The Lune, 2016) with permission

the poetic text with its rendering in Morse code. In both cases, the text is pregnant with information, and particularly for one (like me) who doesn't know Morse code. To read the first line of the English text is an exercise in information as surprise.

Ember Amen

In the edges of visible things silent islets reversible seed hinge oft

ego shift reveries raven eye otherself arias simulcast fie ghost

unmasked his open-access sidewalk prayer to breathe our protest a slim naked sum

that is life thundering heart underheard is it not here human as if this late

whisper still invulnerable should rise back-beaten present-borne no ship will rest

remembrance a splinter-thirst demand against wave-split timber arc ember amen

whose taste for woe what common cause oh first unsay unseen leap second waste ethos.

---

from the author and the publisher, LuNaMoPoLiS.

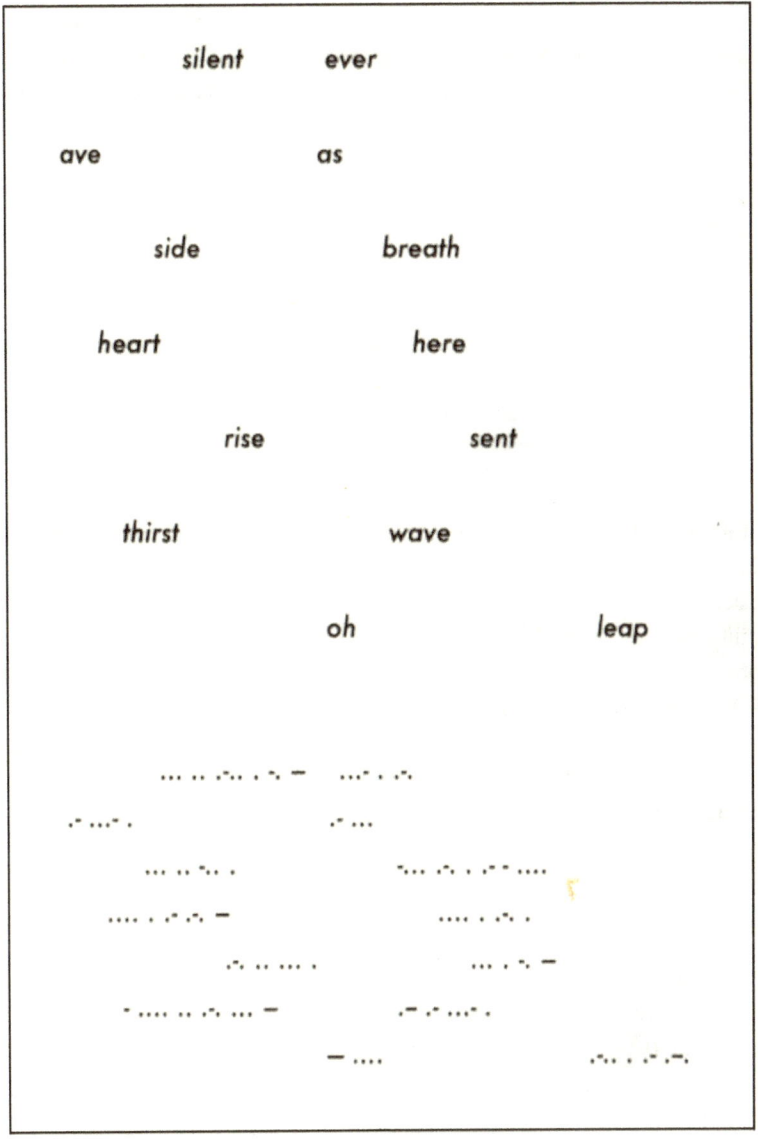

"In the edges of visible things," the poet writes, "silent islets." The message, here, establishes the norms of the code as predictability. In so far as it is understandable, it is also meaningful. The poet continues, however, "reversible seed hinge oft." Here, predictability breaks down and the probability of the code is thrown off kilter. I am left "unhinged." I must—recalling the definition of spinnakers[14]—navigate what comes next with little reliance on

14. "spinnaker, n.," *OED Online*: "A large three-cornered sail carried by racing-yachts,

the code itself.[15] The line in sum can be taken as information rich. The poets dis-order is a disorder in relation to the order of the codes of the English language. The sense that *I* make of the text is one among many senses and is also high in equiprobability. Packed with surprise, the poets text stretches and opens new possibilities for English and, perhaps, Morse.

The information contained within "Ember Amen" cannot be precisely quantified.[16] And, as unquantifiable, information theory morphs into a theory of communication. "Information theory," Eco writes:

> provides us with only one scheme of possible relations . . . as the quantitative measurement of the number of signals that can be clearly transmitted along one channel. Once the signals are received by a human being, information theory has nothing else to add and gives way to either semiology or semantics, since the question henceforth becomes one of signification.[17]

Information theory turned communicative articulates well the role that ambiguity—and what kind of ambiguity—plays in an aesthetics of ambiguity, which uses "conventional linguistic structures to violate the laws of probability that govern the language from within."[18] An aesthetics of ambiguity is concerned with rupture then, a rupture with or departure from the probabilistic linguistic system. This isn't rupture, however, for the sake of rupture or disorder for the celebration of dis-order. Ambiguity pursues rupture to "increase the signifying potential of the message."[19] Conjuring Caglioti,[20] this results in an oscillation "between the institutionalized system of probability and sheer disorder . . . an original organization of disorder."[21]

---

boomed out at right angles to the vessel's side, opposite to the mainsail, and used in running before the wind."

15. Howard, "Ember Amen," 14.
16. Eco, *The Open Work*, 67.
17. Eco, *The Open Work*, 67.
18. Eco, *The Open Work*, 55.

19. It is important to note that an aesthetics of ambiguity is value neutral. It is neither better nor worse than other aesthetic approaches, which Eco clearly articulates elsewhere. What he is concerned with here is showing the particular aesthetics that emerged, within Modernism, from the quantum, chaos, and information revolutions. For other aesthetic approaches, cf. Eco, *The Aesthetics of Chaosmos*; Eco, *On Ugliness*; Eco, *History of Beauty*; Eco, *The Aesthetics of Thomas Aquinas*; Eco, *Art and Beauty in the Middle Ages*.

20. I am aware that Caglioti wrote after Eco. What I am "conjuring" here is the first chapter of this work, not Caglioti's influence on Eco.

21. Eco, *The Open Work*, 63.

Information theory is helpful in defining an aesthetics of ambiguity as a violation of the rules of the code. While this makes sense of aesthetics as a reflection on art, how does it engage aesthetics as sense perception? The second aspect of an aesthetics of ambiguity considers the interpretation of any message as happening within a context. This leads to a "transactional rapport" between a percept and the world of the receiver "that constitutes the very process of perception and reasoning."[22] The world of the receiver or cultural patterns or cultural encyclopedia are not given, they are learned. They are useful assumptions about reality that facilitate the construction of reality and, hence, embodiment in the world. These cultural patterns that facilitate cognition's analysis and integration of perception can be likened to a code. The role of an aesthetics of ambiguity regarding sense perception is to create a space in which a given set of cultural patterns can evolve, be interpreted, and exploited.[23]

Perception is also conceived of as probability in an aesthetics of ambiguity, in so far as any percept is only a "temporary stabilization of a sensible configuration resulting from the more or less redundant organization of useful information that the receiver has selected from a field of stimuli during the perceptual process."[24] A receiver *selects* from a probable field and could, in fact, select otherwise. An aesthetics of ambiguity as sense perception sets out to highlight that which is otherwise, again, not with a *telos* of rupture, but so that any given cultural system can potentially stretch, grow, evolve, and, most importantly, be revealed as a selection. The aesthetics of ambiguity results in perception being a "form of commitment" in that there are "different ways in which one can commit oneself or refuse to commit oneself."[25] As radical as this may sound, within the sphere of an aesthetics of ambiguity, perception itself, perception understood as commitment, is a kind of implicit religion, which defines its subject matter as the various conscious or subconscious "commitments" that I hold and embody in the world.[26]

Ambiguity as a violation of the rules of the code has two important consequences for the study of aesthetics and religion as I have defined it. One, ambiguity ruptures and then expands any given cultural code. Two, ambiguity defines perception as commitment or implicit religion. In both cases, ambiguity is similar to Plate's skinscape, that liminal space between perception and my cultural representations of it. If the skinscape is the

22. Eco, *The Open Work*, 71.
23. Eco, *The Open Work*, 79.
24. Eco, *The Open Work*, 81.
25. Eco, *The Open Work*, 82.
26. Bailey, "Implicit Religion," 271–78.

foundation of the construction of social-sacred spaces, then an aesthetics of ambiguity extends the skinscape's scope, and views ambiguity as the foundation of all constructions of reality, not just the sacred.

But this raises the question: Is all of perception implicitly religious?

Silly, perhaps, but this question probes the boundaries of religion[27] and the ways in which it is utilized within cognition to order perceptions. Religion, on one hand, can be seen as a semiotic system or schema that is influential in the ordering of reality. It can also be, through embodiment and ritual, the very means by which a semiotic or schema is constructed. But in so far as one perceives an oscillating percept and then decides upon a category to place it within—because of different schemata, embodied experiences, or the creation of new knowledge—religion, as I have defined it, is indeed a foundation of perception.[28]

Recall my definition(s) of religion that I articulated in Chapter One, which in itself cannot be sundered from my understanding of aesthetics. Aesthetics distend into both everyday experiences and the creative accounts of experience that humans manufacture to make meaning. Religion is a celebration (both semiotic and embodied) of a communal narrative that is *committedly* lived in the subjunctive—"as if." It is a commitment that one makes to the self and the world, to the semiosphere and the material. Religious aesthetics, and particularly when understood in light of an aesthetics of ambiguity, examines the *meaning making processes*—the commitments and narratives—of humans, grounded in the everyday, taking into consideration the unknowable more of experience. That which is given, in other words, can never be exhausted by my interpretation of it.

27. A definition that includes all things, defines no thing.

28. Cf. An interesting case is that of Saba Mahmood who had her liberal, cultural assumptions challenged while embedded with an Islamic women's group in Egypt. While she would have assumed that the women in question would have wanted to shuck off the authoritative Islamic discursive tradition, she found quite the opposite. Within this environment, Mahmood posed the question: must freedom entail action as a consequence of individual will rather than that of custom, tradition, or social concern? Her answer is that agency must be detached from the goals of progressive politics. "If the ability to effect change in the world and in oneself is historically and culturally specific," Mahmood writes, "then the meaning and sense of agency cannot be fixed in advance . . . [agency] can be understood only from within the discourses and structures of subordination that create the conditions of its enactment." It is important, she continues, to account for a desire that submits to recognized authority. Regarding ambiguity, this poses an interesting question. Can a violation of the rules of the code result in a reification of tradition? As far as Eco is concerned, the answer is no. In Mahmood's case, the ambiguity is present not in her subjects of study, but within her own shift towards a critique of her liberal, free, and Western position. Ambiguity, in other words, must violate the code and, in doing so, open it up to new possibilities. It cannot reject that which is new in favor of tradition. Saba Mahmood, *Politics of Piety*, 14–15.

My version of religious aesthetics, it must be stressed, however, is neither a universal nor a last word. It is only and ever a provisional exploration into the meanings that humans create.

Given these qualifications, perception itself, within the fold of an aesthetics of ambiguity, is most certainly an implicit religion that produces coexistent incompatibilities.

The Composer: Part II
The Interview between Ed and the Author of "The Composer," Diletsky

Diletsky: You have to understand, what Martynov did was unheard of. No one expected it. Why? That's the question. Why invent only to destroy?

Abernathy: And you don't have a good answer to that question?

Diletsky: No. Not really. I researched. Compiled. But could never answer that most basic question, at least not fully. Kseniya thought she had an answer, but it was ultimately of little worth.

Abernathy: Martynov's daughter?

Dilestky: Granddaughter. His only living relative still alive when I was conducting my research. According to her, he knew his ability to compose was derivative. Perhaps it was the anxiety of influence, as one of yours says. And who could blame him. Korsakov. Stravinsky. Borodin. Men of genius. Who would want to follow them?

And so Kseniya, her idea, was that Martynov sought to be remembered the only way he could — through infamy. But that doesn't make sense. By all accounts, it really was the most beautiful, and beautifully structured, composition in history. Rubinstein was there. You can still find his journal online, circulating the conspiracy websites.

Abernathy: Yeah, I read that. "An unknown force," he wrote, "illuminated by the Creator." Strong words, no doubt, but everyone spoke that way. Religion and art were mixed up back then.

Dilestky: But aren't they still? We have a different palate today, no doubt, but it's neither better nor worse. It only is. Rubinstein was a critic with no vested interest in Martynov. Why lie?

Abernathy: That's the question. But if there was one loophole in your book, and forgive me for being so blunt, then it's certainly the question of memory.

Dilestky: I see you've read Thomson. He hated my book. Perhaps people only remembered it that way, perhaps it was the act and not the music they recalled.

Abernathy: Compelling argument.

Dilestky: But wrong. We all order our experiences, file them away. And memory, no doubt, participates in that ordering. It even manipulates it. That cannot be refuted. But to say that an entire audience remembered the thing in only one way or even participated in some kind of musical hoax is just silly.

Abernathy: So if you disagree with Kseniya and Thomson, what's your theory?

Dilestky: You read my book. It's a simple thing, really. Martynov preceded Bulgakov.

Abernathy: "Manuscripts don't burn."

Dilestky: It's better in Russian, but, yes, that's the gist. Compositions are an arrangement of time, an ordering of experience. That's all that music is. And that's the question that Martynov was examining. Can time, once ordered and arranged, be undone? Can the work exist without the artifact?

Abernathy: I see what you're saying, but it's a bit naive. Without the thing—

Dilestky: Without the thing, we have only the symbol. But symbols matter, as much as the thing. Music is a created order related to the dynamics of the material world. They run in parallel, mutually informing one another.

But you have to remember, Martynov's Russia was not your America. You believed in the power of something as simple as a flag. In Russia, it was a different story.

Chernyshevskii spread his grand materialism before he was banished to Siberia, by touting the power of the object. Martynov was trying to transcend that, to say something about the inescapable more.

You're a writer?

Abernathy: Yes.

Dileskty: Have you ever read a book and been so deeply moved by its resonance that you asked yourself—resonance with what?

Abernathy: Not in those words, no, but I understand what you're saying.

Dileskty: And perhaps that's the mystery of art. It's a thing, but not a thing. It's an ordering, but not for all time. It shapes reality, but not the reality into which it was given. It is both thing and not thing.

Abernathy: A paradox of positivism, then?

Dileskty: You might say that, yes. But I prefer to think of Martynov's gesture as a window into reality. A glimpse into the world as it is. The audience created the movement that they wanted outside the constraints of the already known, a known to which they could no longer visit—and then they lived it. That was Martynov's gift.

Encyclopedia and Aesthetics

Imagine that you're an alien visiting Earth from Tau Ceti. You've learned the language as best you can (English, in this case, as you're touring New York), a bit about the various cultures of Earth, and the Terran situation regarding science, politics, and economics (though, frankly, the wanton killing of the human race by the human race is something that strikes you as primitive). Your guide in this smorgasbord of sight and sound decides that you need to experience Yankee Stadium with an accompanying Coney dog—mustard and onions piled high.

As you stride to your seat, secreting your happiness pheromones, you see a woman wearing a large neckless. This isn't the first neckless you've seen of this sort and, in fact, you've been meaning to ask your guide what this particular pattern signifies. Why do people wear that perpendicular line segment? Your guide struggles to answer, to explain her foreign mythology. You smile and nod in appreciation, though very little of what she, your guide, explains makes sense to you.

That night, you lie awake in the bed provided you by the U.N., staring at the ceiling. There is a perpendicular line segment, you think, that humans wear around their necks to signify a cultural myth. Neither the object nor myth compute, you realize, because you have no existing categories on Tau Ceti. To describe what your guide shared would require definition, category, and interpretation, none of which you are equipped to provide. But this is something that your hivemind will want to know about. What can you say? That an object, hammered in silver, is also a myth? That makes little sense.

You turn over and over in your mind the possibilities, thinking through all of the implications. It can't be helped, in the end. You have to submit a report and submit a report you shall. It's up to you then, to render this conundrum understandable. You will have to define, categorize, and interpret. You'll ask your guide for help, but ultimately, it's your responsibility to present the hivemind with something substantial. Yes, you think, it's your job to create meaning.

While it is a contemporary commonplace to refrain from speaking on behalf of the other to provide space for cultural differences, to allow the other to define her own terms, and to acknowledge the reality of privilege (and particularly when it comes to defining *things*)—ambiguity is value neutral. The percept or signifier is itself given as a Firstness (of which more will be said in the following chapters) that can only mean when situated within an already given semiosphere or encyclopedia that has yet to categorize the encountered object. And while it is a moral issue as to whether the perceiver bends to the definition and categorization of the other, ambiguity, frankly, doesn't care.

The possibility exists that, upon sorting the object into a schema, the observer's knowledge about the world changes and grows by expanding into new, previously unconceived of territories. The possibility also exists, however, that the signification of the object—the code by which it arrives at meaning—reifies existing cultural units and interpretants, resulting in little exchange of information. The code can either change or solidify, and ambiguity is only a moment in time, fractions of a second in some cases, in which a perceiver intuits, comprehends, and then chooses.

Codes, in other words, are not stable, and as they stretch or strengthen so too the objects of which they make sense. Here I am interested in the ways that codes expand when confronted with violation and asking the questions: Is the possibility for a violation of the code "written" into the object or does the percept's culture or promulgator confer ambiguity upon it? Is an encountered percept intentionally meant to violate the code or is rupture only a mere happenstance?

In *Semiotics and the Philosophy of Language*, Eco, in an effort to move away from the idea of code (dictionary) and toward the more robust concept of the encyclopedia, asks: Is a definition an interpretation?[29] This question is at the heart of the distinction between a dictionary and encyclopedia. If a sign is something that not only stands for something else but also demands interpretation (a sign is never a given), then a sign also implies inference or, better, Peircean abduction.[30] Given a case, percept, or sign, in other words, I must find its correlating rule. So much of Eco's *The*

---

29. Eco, *Semiotics and the Philosophy of Language*, 46.

30. Peirce's abduction is an inferential process of fashioning a hypothesis to account for a state of affairs. See: Moriarty, "Abduction: A Theory of Visual Interpretation," 167–187; Peirce, *Philosophical Writings of Peirce*, 50–156; Peirce, *Essays in the Philosophy of Science*, 126–143 and 235–255; Eco and Sebeok, *The Sign of Three*, 204.

Name of the Rose is an exploration of this very idea. The dictionary, which aims at correspondence, direct reference, and difference,[31] ultimately fails because it seeks to reduce inference by articulating a finite set of universals, which proves to be an impossible task.[32] If *ram* means male sheep, then one is not only in the uncomfortable position of providing a definition for *sheep* but also clearly identifying a strategy for arriving at a finite set of first terms—those terms that establish the ground for meaning. This leads to the inevitable paradox that "either the [first terms] cannot be interpreted, and one cannot explain the meaning of a term, or they can and must be interpreted, and one cannot limit their number."[33]

Another way of articulating the difference between the dictionary (code) and the encyclopedia is found in *From the Tree to the Labyrinth*. Where the dictionary accounts for analytic properties, those that are necessary and sufficient to distinguish one concept from another, the encyclopedia includes knowledge of the world.[34] As an example, the dictionary, under the heading "dog" would include "animal," "mammal," and "canine," but it would not "assign to the dog the properties of barking or being domesticated."[35] Accounting for knowledge of the world then is one of the distinguishing markers of an encyclopedia, and one of the primary reasons why it, as a cultural universe, is a useful metaphor for an aesthetics of ambiguity.

Rather than correspondence, reference, and difference then, an encyclopedia "assumes that the representation of the content takes place only by means of interpretants, in a process of unlimited semiosis."[36] The content or entry into the encyclopedia is a cultural unit or "anything that is culturally defined and distinguished as an entity.[37] The cultural unit <<dog>> is comprised of an entry, in my culture, that includes <<K-9>>, <<Snoopy>>, and even <<Snoop Dog>>, the American rapper.[38] And what, exactly, is an interpretant or unlimited semiosis, both ideas taken from Peirce?

A sign, according to Peirce, "is something which stands to somebody for something in some respect or capacity." An interpretant is that which

31. Eco, *From the Tree*, 8.
32. Eco, *Semiotics*, 49–68.
33. Eco, *Semiotics*, 57.
34. Eco, *From the Tree*, 3.
35. Eco, *From the Tree*, 3.
36. Eco, *Semiotics*, 68.
37. Eco, *A Theory*, 67.

38. Throughout *A Theory*, Eco uses distinguishing marks to clarify that which he is currently discussing. //xxxx// is the object corresponding to the verbal expression /xxxx/, and both refer to the content unit <<xxxx>>. In other words, //object//, /word/, <<content>>. Cf. *A Theory*, xi.

mediates the "standing for" relationship.[39] It is "another sign translating and explaining the first one, and so on *ad infinitum*."[40] While this processes or movement of unlimited semiosis jumps outward from interpretant to interpretant, it is important to recall that this leap does not tell us something *else* about the sign (which is the criticism that Eco leveled against Derrida),[41] but rather *something more*. To start with <<dog>> and arrive at an American rap artist, in other words, does not imply that I am signifying something else (even though <<Snoop Dog>> has its own set of interpretants). This movement, rather, tells me something more about <<dog>> by articulating difference and expanding both its contents and capabilities or, perhaps, the starting content's cultural purchase or world knowledge. To clarify, the interpretant is not the interpreter of a sign. It is that which guarantees the "validity of the sign, even in the absence of the interpreter."[42]

Getting back to the encyclopedia then, each entry is a cultural unit that is circumscribed by interpretants, a series of clarifications that is continually in flux. Through unlimited semiosis, I can begin with one cultural unit and, given a string of interpretants, arrive at any other cultural unit. This is not an infinite play or regression but a clarifying process that tells me something more about the cultural unit from which I started.

The encyclopedia is the universe of human culture and structured like a labyrinth,[43] which is "a network of interpretants" that is "virtually infinite"[44] that "does not register only 'truths' but, rather, what has been said about the truth or what has been believed to be true as well as what has been believed to be false or imaginary or legendary, provided that a given culture had elaborated some discourse about some subject matter."[45] Within the encyclopedia then is both <<unicorn>> and <<gravity>>, the former of which exists and is true not as a brute fact arising from experience but as a content unit within Western culture. A cultural encyclopedia can never be exhausted. "It is the sum total of everything," in fact, "ever said by humankind."[46]

The encyclopedia is the semiotic world by which any given culture organizes its percepts (fictional ones included). It is flexible, fluid, and nimble.

39. Eco, *A Theory*, 15.
40. Eco, *A Theory*, 15.
41. Eco, *The Limits of Interpretation*, 23–44.
42. Eco, *A Theory*, 68.
43. Eco, *From the Tree*, 53.
44. Eco, *Semiotics*, 83.
45. Eco, *Semiotics*, 84 and *From the Tree*, 26.
46. Eco, *From the Tree*, 49.

It exists as a vast, ever changing network.[47] But it also, locally,[48] has the potential to assume a given tradition, or a "that's just the way it's always been" attitude. When a local encyclopedia seeks global applicability, an ideological bias is produced.[49] Though, of course, global biases can and do exist. It is whenever an encyclopedia is taken as natural—no longer dexterous—that an aesthetics of ambiguity rears its head. "Sometimes," Eco writes, "a poetic text aims at destroying exactly our most unchallengeable assumptions."[50] If information theory defined ambiguity as a violation of the rules of the code, then the encyclopedia defines ambiguity as a challenge to cultural assumptions.[51] As an example, at least in America, one need only think of "The Laramie Project,"[52] "Brokeback Mountain,"[53] or "Angels in America"[54] in reference to the cultural units <<love>>, <<marriage>>, or <<deviant>>.[55]

You will notice, no doubt, that I just committed the cardinal sin of academia. I cited Wikipedia. Why? Because it's the closest material artifact that I have to a global encyclopedia. It is a network of cultural units and interpretants (hyperlinks) that is in constant flux and, at any given time, represents a sum of our *cultural*, as opposed to specialized, knowledge. It is that to which we defer and, in many ways, abdicate our cultural knowing.[56] Do I, in other words, have to know what "The Demi-Virgin" is or can I leave it to Wikipedia to store the cultural knowledge that awaits my recall?[57] With a mission to

---

47. Eco, *From the Tree*, 37.

48. Eco, *From the Tree*, 52.

49. For more on the many levels of Eco's encyclopedia, as well as the role of the subject within any encyclopedia, see: Violi, "Individual and Communal Encyclopedias," 25–38 and "The Subject is in the Adverbs," 113–126. Cf. Eco, *From the Tree*, 70–4.

50. Eco, *Semiotics*, 85 and *From the Tree*, 38.

51. Eco, *From the Tree*, 62.

52. Wikipedia contributors, "The Laramie Project," https://en.wikipedia.org/wiki/The_Laramie_Project.

53. Wikipedia contributors, "Brokeback Mountain," https://en.wikipedia.org/wiki/Brokeback_Mountain.

54. Wikipedia contributors, "Angels in America," https://en.wikipedia.org/wiki/Angels_in_America:_A_Gay_Fantasia_on_National_Themes.

55. To be crystal clear, I am *not* calling homosexuals "deviant," but rather articulating how an encounter with an aesthetic text has the potential to break one out of a cultural paradigm in which "deviance" is equated with the LGBTQ community. In this light, civil rights activism is an exercise in either breaking the circumscribing interpretants of a given cultural unit or creating new links that serve a more ethical end.

56. Eco, *From the Tree*, 93.

57. Wikipedia contributors, "The Demi-Virgin," https://en.wikipedia.org/wiki/The_Demi-Virgin.

gather all recorded knowledge,[58] Wikipedia is a cultural encyclopedia that is dynamic and unstable. It serves as a reminder that "reality cannot be pinned down with finality."[59] This is true, too, for the encyclopedia, which is both a collection of cultural experiences and a schema for ordering that which is continually in a fluid process of movement, reordering, and emergence. It can only be stable upon synchronic reflection. It is an ever-changing representation of a reality that is, even now, recreating itself every moment—established and policed by a swarming team of contributors.

To imagine Eco's encyclopedia as a kind of digitized, crowd-sourced network existing in the cloud[60] is to also pretend that each entry or page on Wikipedia is a cultural unit. The hyperlinks existing within that entry together with its disambiguation can be likened to the interpretants circumscribing that cultural unit. I can begin at Maimonides and, seventeen tabs later, arrive at "The Philosophy of Time." The idiosyncratic nature of the digitized encyclopedia is that the tabs between the one and the other might exist as interpretants only for me. But if they exist for me, then they must also exist as cultural potentialities at which anyone, given the infinity of Babel, could arrive.[61] The encyclopedia as network or labyrinth is moved through or navigated via conjecture, a series of idiosyncratic hypotheses and inferences. And with any new set of connections a polydimensional network of possibility is created that "does not leave unaffected the collective encyclopedia."[62] The individual affects the global.

Thus far, I see two depictions of ambiguity in Eco. One is as a violation of the rules of the code. The other is as a challenge to the assumptions of a given culture. Both cases imply a dis-order or rupture. Ambiguity is an encounter with that which, though relying on a preexistent order (code or encyclopedia), allows me either to see something new in the preexistent order, an opening, or to create something altogether unforeseen from the matter of that which came before. It is an opening, however, that does not necessarily lead to either.

Ambiguity as coexistent incompatibility is slightly different from either violation or challenge. Coexistent incompatibilities highlight the superposition, if I can unabashedly borrow that word from the sciences, of an encounter with an aesthetic object. It is less a violation or challenge and

58. Cf. Eco, *From the Tree*, 49.

59. Gleick, *The Information*, 398.

60. And the cloud is, of course, a material entity.

61. Wikipedia contributors, "The Library of Babel," https://en.wikipedia.org/wiki/The_Library_of_Babel.

62. Eco, *From the Tree*, 69.

more of an awareness of the potentialities of cognition and interpretation. As such, it has the potential to expose the rules by which any culture collapses, from a plurality, into a univocality. Ambiguity as coexistent incompatibility re-articulates Plate's skinscape as not only that which is liminal, but also as a space of sought-after uncertainty. It is that place in which I refrain from judgment. It is the space of the blinking cursor on Wikipedia's search bar that beckons to an infinity of *a posteriori* possibility, in between choice and encounter, order and disorder. It is a hesitation in the face of a potentiality that can either expand or constrict.

Semiotics and Ambiguity

"The aim of [*A Theory of Semiotics*]," Eco ambitiously writes, "is to explore the theoretical possibility and the social function of a unified approach to every phenomenon of signification and/or communication."[63] Broken into three parts: the first deals with signification and communication or how semiotics is a useful methodology for theories of communication. The second espouses a theory of codes. The third elucidates a theory of sign production. The overarching contribution of *A Theory* to the study of semiotics is its insistence that a sign is not a thing but rather a process.[64] Semiotics is not the study of signs, but sign-functions, which results in a distinction between communication and signification, between "things said" and "things meant."[65] A thing said is a produced sign. A thing meant is interpreted against the backdrop of the encyclopedia.

The first section of *A Theory* defines sign-function, as opposed to the static notion of a "sign." A sign-function is realized when expression and content enter into a mutual correlation.[66] This is in contrast to a sign—everything which can be taken as significantly substituting for something else[67]—which is "always an element of an *expression plane* conventionally correlated to one (or several) elements of a *content plane*."[68] Given these distinctions, a semiotics of *signification* entails a theory of codes and encyclopedias, while a semiotics of *communication* entails a theory of sign-production. Signification, in other words, necessarily relates to the cultural code and the way in which I decode any given message, while communication is concerned with

63. Eco, *A Theory*, 3.
64. Eco, *A Theory*, 152.
65. Eco, *The Name of the Rose*, 316.
66. Eco, *The Name of the Rose*, 49.
67. Eco, *The Name of the Rose*, 7.
68. Eco, *A Theory*, 48.

the various ways in which a society or person constructs or creates its signs. Semiotics, in this non-Saussurean school, views all cultural processes as processes of communication or sign-production.

A communicative process is the passage of a signal from a source to a destination. A signification system is an autonomous semiotic construct that has an abstract mode of existence independent of any possible communicative act it makes possible. "Every act of communication to or between human beings," Eco writes, "presupposes a signification system as its necessary condition."[69] To communicate, in other words, is to assume that there is a probabilistic code or encyclopedia by which any message can be decoded or understood.

The process of decoding is synonymous with sign-function, which is realized whenever an expression and a content are in mutual correlation. It is the code or encyclopedia (usually, if not always cultural) that establishes the correlation.[70] This is an important point as it makes abundantly clear that an expression does not have a referent.[71] It has, rather, a content, which exists in the code of culture (encyclopedia) and is realized in cultural units.[72] And, as already suggested, it is cultural units that are "circumscribed" by Peircean interpretants[73]... and "provide the conditions for a complex interplay of sign-functions."[74]

Though I have already introduced cultural units via <<dog>>, it is necessary to reiterate or more fully articulate the cultural unit here. If //automobile//[75] is the car or object that corresponds to the verbal expression /automobile/, then both refer to the content or cultural unit <<automobile>>. While this example is straightforward, it is important to remember that the content of <<automobile>> contains within it *all* that *could* go into an exhaustive (perhaps infinite) entry into a cultural encyclopedia. It would include not only //automobiles// but also their interpretants or those entries in the encyclopedia that are connected to the entry on //automobiles//, even if only tangentially (think of my previous discussion on Wikipedia).[76] While

69. Eco, *A Theory*, 8–9.
70. Eco, *A Theory*, 50.
71. Eco, *A Theory*, 58.
72. Eco, *A Theory*, 61 and 67.
73. Eco, *A Theory*, 68–69.
74. Eco, *A Theory*, 56.

75. Throughout *A Theory*, Eco uses distinguishing marks to clarify that which he is currently discussing. //xxxx// is the object corresponding to the verbal expression /xxxx/. Both refer to the content unit <<xxxx>>. In other words, //object//, /word/, <<content>>. Cf. Eco, *A Theory*, xi.

76. Like when an entry ends with, "see also."

the example of the //automobile// is in no way flashy, imagine the West's cultural unit or encyclopedic entry on //Jesus// and all the other entries that it might connect to. What is important to remember is that neither //Jesus// nor /Jesus/ refers to the concrete historical figure of the first-century Mediterranean world (whoever that may be), but rather the content comprising its entry in the encyclopedia. //Jesus//, in other words, refers not to that which is "actual" but to <<Jesus>>, its cultural content, which is circumscribed by a swirling network of interpretants or other, similar entries (cultural units) in the cultural encyclopedia.

Finally, what is the act of communication or sign production and how does it connect to signs, encyclopedias, and an aesthetics of ambiguity? Utterances aim to communicate and are acts of labor. To produce a signal one must first isolate and choose an expression-unit and then connect that unit, coherently (in so far as it aligns with any given culture's coding or encyclopedia), to an expression-string.[77] What is important here is that codes and encyclopedias (things meant) are in service to sign production (things said), which—together—are in service to semiotics as a socio-cultural process. Cultural codes tell me what expressions and contents (cultural units) I can and cannot match up for the purposes of sign production or concrete communication. Though, as I have already shown, the idea of a cultural code is far more fluid and flexible when conceived of as a cultural encyclopedia.

There are three ways in which a sign can be produced: one, by shaping the expression-continuum; two, by correlating that shaped continuum with its possible content; and three, by connecting these newly produced signs to factual events, things, or states of the world.[78] The aesthetic text, which I am primarily concerned with, is a manipulation of the expression-plane with the intended result being a reassessment of the content-plane.[79] I speak poetically to call into question the encyclopedia.

This "aesthetic sign-function," Eco writes, "is based . . . [on] a process of code changing."[80] One can study aesthetic texts to study all the aspects of sign-functions: "It can perform any or all productive functions . . . and it can require any kind of productive labor."[81] But what makes an aesthetic text an aesthetic text? The fact that it's ambiguous and self-focusing. Ambiguity is "a mode of violating the rules of the code," which is rooted in information theory, or forcing the "hearer to reconsider the entire organization of the

77. Eco, *A Theory*, 151.
78. Eco, *A Theory*, 157.
79. Eco, *A Theory*, 261.
80. Eco, *A Theory*, 261.
81. Eco, *A Theory*, 261.

content," which is rooted in the encyclopedia.[82] Ambiguity, as I have already suggested, is both a violation of and challenge to the codes and encyclopedias of culture. In *A Theory*, and here is Eco's third essential aspect of ambiguity, what is violated or challenged is the *expression-content correlation*.[83]

In sum, a theory of sign production is communicative. It is that message which moves from a sender through a channel to a receiver. It is not yet a signification (a thing meant), as that begins only once a message has been received *and* begun to be interpreted. Ambiguity as coexistent incompatibility is interested in things meant or the process of interpretation after encountering a percept. It is only, it seems to me, concerned with things said when, along with Winkler, it begins to ask questions about where ambiguity occurs—in the production or perception of a percept.

Communication systems (things said) have rules for combining and manipulating those messages that travel from sender or source to receiver or destination. This is a "syntactic system,"[84] which provides a structure "to communicative acts that limit the range of possible interpretations an addressee can give to a message."[85] To create a message is to participate in four types of sign producing labor: recognition, ostension, replica, and invention. I am here, however, only concerned with the latter.[86] Invention relates to a producer of a sign-function choosing "a new way of organizing existing expression units" and then seeking to make her new way of correlation acceptable.[87] When it comes to ambiguity, the labor of invention proposes novel ways of cultural organization. In Winkler's language, this means that Echian ambiguity when considered as an act of communication is strategically produced and potentially enables the receiver to "view the world in a way different from the standard ways of viewing."[88] This is akin to Victor Shklovsky's defamiliarization[89] and is a deliberate violation and challenge to bring attention both to the nature of the code and encyclopedia.[90]

82. Eco, *A Theory*, 262–63.
83. Eco, *A Theory*, 264.
84. Eco, *A Theory*, 49.
85. Eco, *A Theory*, 49.
86. Recognition relates to a pre-existing and coded physical correlation. Ostention relates to taking an object as an example of the class of which it is a member. Replica relates to referring "to items that can be replicated and intentionally produced and reproduced in order to signify." These can be phonemes and morphemes or flags and musical notes. See, Radford, *On Eco*, 54.
87. Radford, *On Eco*, 54.
88. Radford, *On Eco*, 54.
89. Shklovsky, "Art As Technique," 775–84.
90. Cf. Radford, *On Eco*, 55.

This leads me to the final piece of this chapter's puzzle regarding Eco's ambiguity. As an introduction to the aesthetic experience, it produces further knowledge because it "compels one to reconsider the usual codes and their possibilities."[91] This "further knowledge" is ascertained by "aesthetic abduction," proposing tentative codes—what I previously referred to as conjecture—to make the author's message understandable but which the reader will not know directly.[92]

I have codes out of which I operate. I take these codes for granted. From these codes, messages are produced, received, embodied, and reified, only to be once again produced. This is the process of culture as Eco envisions it, a process that can be arrested, interrogated, and restructured through ambiguity. And it is through the latter process that any given cultural code or encyclopedia can be rearranged or interrogated, and then said to have produced a knowledge that was previously unthinkable.

If I can make one further distinction or clarifying remark regarding ambiguity's potential for the creation of further knowledge, then it comes in the guise of ideology. The messages that any sign producer constructs propagates "coded ideologies," which are the labors of "selecting and preferring one worldview over another."[93] Ideological labor is a difficult work that "has to be actively performed on a potentially problematic reality."[94] If I am dissatisfied with the current state of the political order, then I could labor to confer an alternate view of the world upon that which I see, which would allow me to generate my privileged interpretation over against others. But an ideological interpretation is always *a partial interpretation* of the world.[95] It is a message that starts with a factual description "and then tries to justify it theoretically, gradually being accepted by society through a process of overcoding."[96]

Perhaps I can say it this way: Ideologies force a particular reading (univocality) while ambiguity allows for possible readings (plurivocality). This is, of course, what interests me the most in the notion of an aesthetics of ambiguity, which, given a "text" or percept, creates a liminal space of possibility—readings and interpretations that not only violate, challenge, and create further knowledge on the plane of expression, but also account for, by arresting judgment, coexistent incompatibilities—the infinite probability of an uncollapsed superposition.

---

91. Eco, *A Theory*, 274.
92. Eco, *The Limits of Interpretation*, 140.
93. Radford, *On Eco*, 56.
94. Radford, *On Eco*, 58.
95. Eco, *A Theory*, 289.
96. Eco, *A Theory*, 290. I will explore this much further in Part II.

Conclusion

Information theory defines ambiguity as a violation of the rules of the code. The encyclopedia highlights ambiguity's ability to challenge our cultural assumptions. And the semiotics of Eco reveal the potential of ambiguity to create further knowledge. These distinctions allow me to delineate further what I mean by coexistent incompatibility and how it is both informed by but different from Eco's ambiguity. For me, ambiguity is a space wherein I refrain from judgment so that I can more fully acknowledge the plurivocality or potentiality of a given percept. It is an encounter with that which forces upon me the factuality of many, equiprobable realities. Ambiguity does not, however, provide a way forward. It is neither map nor guide. It is a hesitancy, a refusal to judge or, better yet, a position from which one can foresee the infinite possibilities of a possible future.

Whereas Plate speaks of the skinscape, a mediating position halfway between the semiosphere and the material world, perhaps I am articulating a nodal point in a network. From there, I can foresee the many, possible paths of traversal without yet committing to one over against another. All are coexistent but, once chosen, incompatible. A material aesthetic informed by an ambiguity seen as coexistent incompatibility would begin to articulate the possibility, given a set of cultural probabilities, that any percept—at the point of perception—potentially holds. A material aesthetic informed by ambiguity would not view religious objects, rituals, or embodiments as univocalities. To do so, like von Balthasar, would be a labor of ideology. Ambiguity, in my estimation, is concerned with the ways in which material aesthetics not only views or engages its subject matter as instances of violation, challenge, or further knowledge on the plane of expression, but also as a coexistent incompatibility that has the potential either to create or highlight religious commitments and narratives—implicit religion—as they mutually exist as polyvocal percepts. A material aesthetic rooted in ambiguity would not only examine this phenomenon but also those narratives that allow any observer to choose one vocality over another.

In the epigraph of this chapter, I referenced Alan Moore's *Jerusalem*. Written over the course of a decade, Moore's novel is well over 1200 pages in length. Daunting to most, if not all, readers, his book was published to critical acclaim, being compared to both James Joyce and Cormac McCarthy.[97] Chronicling the life of Northampton's Boroughs, *Jerusalem* is jam-packed with many a tale sprawling from the middle ages of England to the not so distant future. Its protagonists are varied and, depending upon the chapter, tell the story of a Victorian housewife or a prostitute in the 2000s. Early

---

97. Sheehan, "'Jerusalem' Is Alan Moore's Really Big Book."

on, Moore writes of Ernest Vernall,[98] an artist in 1865 commissioned with touching up the frescoes in St. Paul's Cathedral. It is no ordinary day for Ern, however, as it is the day he is destined—like his father before him—to lose his sanity.[99] "The fresco," Moore writes, "that Ern planned to clean up and retouch . . . was one that he was not familiar with from sermons . . . [he] decided to begin his restorations with a halo-sporting figure in the picture's upper left, angel or saint he couldn't tell."[100]

Beginning with the figure's clothes, Ern soon realizes with horror that the frescoed figure breaks "from the confines of its two-dimensional domain" and turns its massive face towards him.[101] "Jaw hung wide," Ern cannot scream, but only listen as the figure opens its maw and begins to speak an unknown language, but one that Ern can mysteriously comprehend.[102] And what does this figure, this aesthetic event now identified as an angel, communicate to Ern?

> It seemed anxious to convey instruction of profound importance on a staggering range of topics, many of them seeming to be matters of mathematics and geometry for which Ern, though illiterate, had always had a flair. The knowledge, anyway, decanted into him so that he had no choice as to whether he took it in or not . . . the lecture was expansive, introducing Ern to points of view he'd never really thought about before. He was invited to consider time with every moment of its passing in the terms of plane geometry, and had it pointed out that human beings' grasp of space was incomplete.[103]

When all was said and done, Ern came down from the rafters a broken, giggling, and sobbing man. "It was not as though there was no recognition there in his expression," Moore writes, "but more as if he had been away so long that he had come to think his former occupation and companions all a dream."[104]

---

98. And, as Moore reminds us in *Jerusalem*: "A Vernall tended to the boundaries and corners . . . those that bent into the fourth direction . . . Vernalls overlooked the crossroads of two very different planes, sentinels straddling a gulf that no one else could see. As such they would be prone to certain instabilities, yet at the same time often were recipient to more-than-normal insights, talents or capacities," 428.

99. Moore, *Jerusalem*, 43.

100. Moore, *Jerusalem*, 55.

101. Moore, *Jerusalem*, 57.

102. Moore, *Jerusalem*, 57.

103. Moore, *Jerusalem*, 61–62.

104. Moore, *Jerusalem*, 65.

Interpreted through a lens of ambiguity, Ern, the artist, was confronted by an artwork so overwhelmingly powerful that he had no category into which he could receive it. But, as outside of everyday experience as the event was, Ern could neither dismiss it nor pretend that it never happened. He was confronted with all the forms of ambiguity that I have discussed in this chapter. An angel stepping out of a painting, clearly, is a violation of the rules of the code—in this case, the code of Western empiricism. It is also a challenge to the cultural encyclopedia in that, prior to this encounter, Ern could not have conceived of a corresponding interpretant for the entry on "Frescoes." Likewise, the confrontation with the angel created an opening so large in Ern's encyclopedia that further knowledge—new knowledge, in fact—was created or, in this case, decanted into him. But I wonder if all these interpretations cannot be attributed to the real and paradoxical encounter with a coexistent incompatibility. Frescoes do not talk. And, yet, this fresco talks. Given a choice then, a nodal point in a vast network in which all potentials are present because time has collapsed, Ern chose a path of non-integration. That which happened could not happen so, grasping onto his old categories, he chose a link in the network that led to insanity or madness. But, returning to that node, one wonders if perhaps there were no other, potential paths that he could have traversed.

As I previously wrote, ambiguity is concerned with the ways in which aesthetics not only views or engages its subject matter as instances of violation, challenge, or further knowledge, but also as a coexistent incompatibility, which has the potential either to create or highlight implicit religion, commitments and narratives, as they mutually exist as polyvocal percepts. Aesthetic rooted in ambiguity would not only examine this phenomenon but also those narratives that allow any observer to choose one vocality over another. If that is given, then the task when analyzing Ern's encounter not only becomes probing the plurivocality of ambiguity, but also the underlying narratives that led Ern to choose one path over against another, equiprobable path. It is also to claim Ern's position atop the scaffolding, circumscribed by a crumbling dome, as an ambiguous space in which the infinity of possibility has not yet collapsed, for that is the full awareness of ambiguity.

Excursus One
The Dispossessed

> But was not a theory of which all the elements were provably true a simple tautology? In the region of the unprovable, or even the disprovable, lay the only chance for breaking out of the circle and going ahead.
>
> —Ursula K. Le Guin, *The Dispossessed*

Introduction

THE PURPOSE OF THIS excursus is twofold. One, to suggest that science fiction is one of ambiguity's strongest allies. And two, that an aesthetics of ambiguity transcends the work of Umberto Eco. To accomplish these two goals, I examine Ursula K. Le Guin's novel, *The Dispossessed: An Ambiguous Utopia* and argue that ambiguity flourishes in science fiction's potential to comment on the present.

Setting the Scene

> Where, then, is Truth? ... In the hill one happens to be sitting on.[1]

Imagine a future wherein capitalism and socialism are entrenched to such a degree that both parties can no longer inhabit the same planet. And rather than continue their age-old war, the two agree upon a cosmic armistice. The socialists colonize the moon to pursue a communitarian project, but at the expense of never again setting foot on earth.

Consider two-hundred years passing. Neither the moon nor the earth have been in communication. The lunar colony, having created its own language, cultural encyclopedia, and economic system, no longer considers

---

1. Le Guin, *The Dispossessed*, 41.

itself the same race as those who inhabit earth. For the living, the moon is the only home they have ever known.

Picture this new world with all of its idiosyncrasies, differences, and assumptions. It is not our world. It is foreign and strange. It is a culture wherein "family" has no meaning and sex and sexuality are shared and fluid. There is no personal property. Individuality is frowned upon. And intellectual property is not a functioning concept. It is a society that is flawed, no doubt, but one that operates well for its inhabitants.

Now imagine a scientist on that world. He is a theoretical physicist concerned with the nature of time. Working on a theory of simultaneity that stitches together time as arrow and time as circle, he reaches out to earth. He desires to share scientific research, to learn, to grow, and to stretch his epistemological horizon. He not only learns earth's language, but also freely shares his theories. After a time, the scientist decides to visit earth. He hopes to utilize earth's vast resources in order to solve the problem of simultaneity. He is the first and only lunar colonist to return to the home planet.

Ambiguity in fiction—but particularly science fiction—constructs a possible, as-if world in such a way that I experience or see my embodied, narrativizing theory in a new light or from a slanted perspective. While at first glance that which violates, challenges, or expands my horizon is encountered by the strangeness of the lunar world, I wonder if ambiguity is not better understood here as self-reflexive? My encyclopedia grows not only when I interact with the ambiguity of the other—the lunar society and culture—but also when I consider how the other might defamiliarize my already given—how the lunar society and culture envisages me.

Ambiguity is a confrontation with the taken for granted. It allows me to conceive of a world in which things are ordered differently and, in doing so, critique my own ordering or arrangement of realty. What is ambiguous here is not the foreignness of the socialist, lunar colony—though it is that—but rather seeing the earth for the first time through the eyes of the lunar scientist, Shevek.

Science fiction as ambiguity, read through *The Dispossessed*, performs a self-referential task by creating a critical distance between that world and mine. It breaks down the dogmas of the present and allows for the possibility of epistemological provisionality. By entering into an imagined extension of the present, I am able to gain unique insights into what may or may not be. I am able to play with choice and consequence and conceive of alternate ways of being in the world.

Shevek not only encounters ambiguity in his travels—that which violates, challenges, and questions his own encyclopedia—but he also represents ambiguity as self-reflexivity for his readers. And, on a larger scale,

Shevek's genre is uniquely suited for strategically produced ambiguity in that it provides critical distance on the present and functions as a foretelling of what might be.

Crossing the Wall

> Like all walls it was ambiguous, two-faced. What was inside it and what was outside it depended upon which side of it you were on.[2]

A wall separates the lunar colonies from the moon's spaceport. Walls are enigmas, however. When one does not possess, what use are walls? And yet, this wall is more than its material. It represents, among other things, the boundary between encyclopedias, between the lunar social world and earth's. When Shevek crosses that boundary in order to travel to earth, he realizes that "you shall not go down twice to the same river, nor can you go home again."[3] To cross that boundary is, in lunar terms, to become a profiteer and an egoist.

Shevek is neither, of course. He his only hungry for knowledge and intellectual community. But his reception is less than he had hoped for. Befriending the ship's doctor, Shevek asks why the Second Officer is afraid of him. "Oh," the doctor responds, "with him it's religious bigotry. He's a strict-interpretation Epiphanist. Recites the Primes every night. A totally rigid mind." To the Second Officer then, Shevek is ambiguous. He is an event that challenges his encyclopedic arrangement, his narrativizing theory, and, recognizing this, the Second Officer rejects the possibility for ambiguity and self-reflexivity. He rejects provisionality.

This prompts Shevek to ask:

> 'So he [,the Second Officer,] sees me—how?'
> 'As a dangerous atheist.'
> 'An atheist! Why?'
> 'Why, because you're [from the lunar colony], Anarres—there's no religion on Anarres.'
> 'No religion? Are we stones, on Anarres?'
> 'I mean established religion—churches, creeds—' Kimoe [, the doctor,] flustered easily. He had the physician's brisk self-assurance, but Shavek continually upset it. All his explanations ended up, after two or three of Shevek's questions, in

---

2. Le Guin, *The Dispossessed*, 1.
3. Le Guin, *The Dispossessed*, 54.

> floundering. Each took for granted certain relationships that the other could not even see.[4]

What is revealing about this exchange is not necessarily the response of the Second Officer to Shevek, but rather the admission at the end. "Each took for granted," the narrator claims, "certain relationships that the other could not even see." And by "relationships," the narrator is suggesting, to use my language, relationships between cultural units in either's respective encyclopedia, which result in a coexistent incompatibility. For each cultural unit, Shevek and Kimoe not only have different content, but also different interpretants. For both, <<religion>> is not a shared cultural unit, but one that breeds ambiguity, a confrontation with the other's unconceived of referent.

For Shevek:

> Kimoe's ideas never seemed to be able to go in a straight line; they had to walk around this and avoid that, and then they ended up smack against a wall. There were walls around all his thoughts, and he seemed utterly unaware of them, though he was perpetually hiding behind them.[5]

And so, walls return. Here, however, they are not separating cultural encyclopedias, but rather the potentialities of an already given encyclopedia—those connections that one makes leaping from interpretant to interpretant. Shevek is frustrated by Kimoe's inability to navigate the lunar encyclopedia but, consequently, is blind to his own inability to make connections from Kimoe's point of view.

Walls are undoubtedly a repeated theme in *The Dispossessed*, and later represent that which ambiguity must challenge. "Those who build walls," Shevek suggests, "are their own prisoners. I'm going to go fulfill my proper function in the social organism. I'm going to go unbuild walls."[6] Shevek's encounter with ambiguity results in a formulation of the work of ambiguity, which is the shattering of cultural givens, while also facilitating new connections across the cultural network.

---

4. Le Guin, *The Dispossessed*, 14.
5. Le Guin, *The Dispossessed*, 16.
6. Le Guin, *The Dispossessed*, 331.

The Inventor-Destroyer

> Not a craftsman—a creator. An inventor-destroyer, the kind who's got to turn everything upside down and inside out. A satirist, a man who praises through rage.[7]

The lunar colony is a utopia, but an ambiguous one. By that, I think, Le Guin means to imply that the moon's colony, though oxymoronic, isn't a perfect utopia. It is only utopian in that it seeks to correct earth's flaws, but, in doing so, creates its own set of encyclopedic imperfections.

One consequence of the lunar colony's encyclopedia is its cultural inability to acknowledge or recognize humor, satire, or irony, especially when employed in critique of its socialist system. Tirin, a childhood friend of Shevek, is an artist turned satirist. He writes a play that is intended to be a humorous critique of the social system of the lunar colony, but, inevitably, it falls flat. Tirin, before the performance of the play, is said to be "funny" and "alive,"[8] but after he is a broken man forced to live in the moon's therapy colony. And what broke him? "The play broke him."

> 'The play? The Tuss those old turds made about it? Oh, but listen, to be driven crazy by that kind of moralistic scolding you'd have to be crazy already. All he had to do was ignore it!'
> 'Tir was crazy already. By our society's standards.'
> 'What do you mean?'
> 'Well, I think Tir's a born artist. Not a craftsman—a creator. An inventor-destroyer, the kind who's got to turn everything upside down and inside out. A satirist, a man who praises through rage.'[9]

But Tirin is a free colonist, so why not do what he likes and reject what he does not? Perhaps, in his lunar freedom, he could even be the lunar colony's conscience? According to Shevek it is impossible to break free from the already given encyclopedia of culture.

> 'The social conscience completely dominates the individual conscience, instead of striking a balance with it. We don't cooperate—we *obey*. We fear being outcast, being called lazy, dysfunctional, egoizing. We fear our neighbor's opinion more than we respect our freedom of choice . . . We force a man outside the sphere of our approval, and then condemn him for it. We've

---

7. Le Guin, *The Dispossessed*, 327.
8. Le Guin, *The Dispossessed*, 326.
9. Le Guin, *The Dispossessed*, 327.

made laws, laws of conventional behavior, built walls all around ourselves, and we can't see them, because they're part of our thinking... [Tirin] never did it, he never could build walls.'[10]

And so even the lunar colony has an encyclopedia and a narrativized theory that they take for granted, as if. They are incapable of escaping that narrative, because it is muted, hidden in the background. It lives in the darkness of their imagination and disallows genuine innovation. There is no room for lightness of being. Shevek recognizes his culture's low tolerance for ambiguity and understands Tirin's life as an unfortunate consequence of that fact.

Shevek is lucky, however. Even though he is also an innovator, he is provided with more leeway because he is a scientist and not an artist. "A scientist can pretend that his work isn't himself," Shevek says, "it's merely the impersonal truth. An artist can't hide behind the truth. He can't hide anywhere."[11] The scientist hides behind Firstness or capital "F" fact. Science strips *poesis* out of its narrativizing theory. It's not a making. It's that which is. But for the artist and poet, the creative act is a different story.

There is a strong desire in Shevek to enact an aesthetic of ambiguity, which is the desire to peel back the layers of the already given, to question it, and to expose its *as-if-ness*. His is a longing for a provisional epistemology. A knowledge that eschews certainty and dogma for process.[12] It is an acknowledgment that Tirin could not hide, not like a scientist, because he was responsible for both his creation and his choice in mapping a fiction onto reality. But what Shevek points out is that we all—artists and scientists alike—are responsible to and accountable for the creative and reifying choices we make.[13]

The World We Know

> Is there no alternative to selling? Is there not such a thing as the gift?[14]

Shevek encounters ambiguity and desires to enact it. He alludes to breaking walls, coexistent incompatibility, and choice. But Shevek also represents ambiguity for the reader, the possibility of confronting that which she takes

---

10. Le Guin, *The Dispossessed*, 329.
11. Le Guin, *The Dispossessed*, 329–30.
12. Le Guin, *The Dispossessed*, 332.
13. Le Guin, *The Dispossessed*, 224.
14. Le Guin, *The Dispossessed*, 344.

for granted. In his ambiguity, Shevek conjures a world in which things are ordered differently, which allows the reader, self-reflexively, to critique her own ordering—her narrativizing theory.

After flying to the moon's home world, Shevek does his best to learn the cultural signs of high capitalism. Even though his encyclopedia grows as a result of the journey, he is often confused, frustrated, and out of step. The proletariat of the home world, however, see Shevek as a divergent social option, one that overcomes capitalism, servitude, and oppression.

Shevek, to his dismay, unwittingly starts a revolution. He is no longer welcome, yet he cannot return home, for the lunar colony no longer recognizes him as a citizen. What's a cosmic scientist to do, other than seek asylum at the local Terran consulate?

After a lengthy silence, Earth's ambassador turns to Shevek, the man who started a revolution:

> 'We are both aliens here, Shevek,' she said at last. 'I from much farther away in space and time. Yet I begin to think that I am much less alien to Urras than you are ... Let me tell you how this world seems to me. To me, and to all my fellow Terrans who have seen the planet, Urras is the kindliest, most various, most beautiful of all the inhabited worlds. It is the world that comes as close as any could to Paradise.'[15]

That which is repulsive to Shevek, a high capitalism that strips its lower classes of free choice, is a paradise to the Terran ambassador. A clash of narrativizing theories, the two are nearly impossible to reconcile. The perceptions of Shevek and the ambassador are, in fact, coexistent incompatibilities. Where the one sees greed, injustice, and waste, the other sees goodness, beauty, and vitality.[16]

"You man," the ambassador continues, "from a world I cannot even imagine, you who see my Paradise as Hell, will you ask what my world must be like?"[17]

And as the ambassador's question lingers in the air, the self-reflexivity of ambiguity presents itself, too:

> 'My world, my Earth, is a ruin. A planet spoiled by the human species. We multiplied and gobbled and fought until there was nothing left, and then we died. We controlled neither appetite nor violence; we did not adapt. We destroyed ourselves. But we

---

15. Le Guin, *The Dispossessed*, 346.
16. Le Guin, *The Dispossessed*, 346.
17. Le Guin, *The Dispossessed*, 346–47.

destroyed the world first . . . We can only look at this splendid world, this vital society, this Urras, this Paradise, from the outside. We are capable only of admiring it, and maybe envying it a little.'

'Then Anarres, as you heard me speak of it—what would Anarres mean to you, Keng?'

'Nothing. Nothing, Shevek. We forfeited our chance for Anarres centuries ago, before it ever came into being.'[18]

Ambiguity, among other possibilities, is the question that the text poses to its reader. Can you recognize your present in these words?

Conclusion

'What is it like,' she said, 'what can it be like, the society that made you? I heard you speak of Anarres, in the Square, and I wept listening to you, but I didn't really believe you.'[19]

The Dispossessed is a narrative of ambiguity, clashing encyclopedias, and narrativizing theories. It is a work of science fiction that also comments on the present. It illuminates, through Shevek, coexistent incompatibility—the way in which the reader peels back layers of experience in an effort to expose the ordering of the semiosphere. It allows the reader to confront her own encyclopedia, her own present. It reveals the potentiality of provisional thinking, an epistemology that grips loosely, examines self-reflexively, and is given to humility. *The Dispossessed* is representative of ambiguity's process, as well as the alliance that holds between science fiction and the aesthetics of ambiguity.

---

18. Le Guin, *The Dispossessed*, 347–48.
19. Le Guin, *The Dispossessed*, 345.

3
Some Lines Can't Be Crossed

'What a remarkably magical spot!' said Mr Honeyfoot, approvingly. 'Your dream—so full of odd symbols and portents—is yet another proof of it!'

'But what does it *mean*?' asked Mr Segundus.

'Oh!' said Mr Honeyfoot, and stopt to think a while. 'Well, the lady wore blue, you say? Blue signifies—let me see—immortality, chastity and fidelity; it stands for Jupiter and can be represented by tin. Hmmph! Now where does that get us?'

'Nowhere, I think,' sighed Mr Segundus.

—Susanna Clarke, *Jonathan Strange & Mr Norrell*

Introduction

Echoing Mr Segundus and Mr Honeyfoot, I too ask: What does it mean? What do the infinite interpretants that lead to yet another node in the network illuminate? Truth? Being? Or less dramatically, things as they really are? I have argued that in ambiguity defined as a coexistent incompatibility there is no *one* reality. There is, rather, a multiplicity of possibilities that overlie one another and, at any given moment, an individual or a community invents the real by employing an ever fluid, ever dynamic encyclopedia. Another individual or community, however, could choose differently and, as a result, instantiate a reality that exists simultaneously as an entangled universe. What I have articulated then is two states, coexistent and entangled, but mutually incompatible. A recognition of this coexistent incompatibility is the *state* of ambiguity, which is also and often instigated by an *encounter* with that which is ambiguous in an Echian sense: a text that violates the rules of the code or an encounter that challenges cultural assumptions or an event in which further knowledge is produced. In any case, the ambiguous encounter reveals the state of ambiguity as a coexistent incompatibility.

What I wonder and am, in fact, probing throughout this book is if it is possible to employ a non-judgmental aesthetics, defer the collapsing of any superposition, and remain in a state of ambiguity as long as possible. Why would I desire that? Because it seems to me that the longer I remain in a coexistent incompatibility, the longer I have to interrogate the codes, encyclopedias, and semiospheres that confine my ability to judge. As such, I am arguing that aesthetics is a space in which a non-judgmental analysis can take place. I am not only describing Plate's skinscape, but also arguing for an aesthetics of ambiguity that intentionally seeks to remain liminal—between the encyclopedia and the object, semiotics and materiality.

I must stress, however, that this is not a muted form of objectivity. I am not, by articulating the in-between spaces of coexistent incompatibilities, suggesting that one can escape her encyclopedia. I am merely suggesting that by seeking to remain within the skinscape one can better reveal the systems and processes by which she judges and, in doing so, confront the ways in which the other orders and embodies her encyclopedia as an *equally valid instantiation of reality*—irrespective of that reality's ethic. Ambiguity as a coexistent incompatibility is not a way out of subjectivity, but rather an admission that individual and collective representations of reality are the sum of all that is—and furthermore, that those representations are not outside the scope of interrogation.

While this summary of my project might appear to be a full acceptance of a caricaturized poststructuralism, it is, in fact, no such thing. For this chapter argues that any commitment made when encountering a percept is an interpretation that assumes a *that-which-is-to-be-interpreted*. I am arguing, in other words, that there is something that induces us to produce signs, which is no mere simulacrum, let alone an endless chain of simulacra.[1] There is a *thing* but I cannot know it outside the potentialities of my encyclopedia, which exists coextensively with other constructions of reality—or chosen and ordered things. I cannot know it, but it is there, pushing back, instigating my interpretations of it.

The Sense of Sense

I have already discussed the ever-fluid encyclopedia and the way in which it delimits cultural knowing, while also making it possible to produce further knowledge. I am now interested in shifting back to the aesthetics of sense

---

1. Eco, *Kant and the Platypus*, 12.

perception and discussing that which holds the encyclopedia accountable. If that is the wrong word, then perhaps all I mean is the some*thing* that catalyzes the creation of a cultural semiosphere. When I read a text and then interpret it, to put it differently, it is the text that causes or cultivates my interpretation of it. The text induces me to produce an interpretation. I am beholden or accountable to the text in so far as I want to interpret it and not something else. If I take that which induces me and drift widely afield, then I have not interpreted *it* but have, rather, used it.

To summarize by way of example, the text of *Moby Dick* has instigated countless interpretations. It is that something that I could analogously call Being. I must, if I desire to remain faithful to that which presents itself to me, be accountable to it. If I do not, then I am none the worse—but I have not interpreted, I have used.[2] While I could argue at length the reasons why the White Whale represents a pink pansy in the garden of Melville, I would be using the text and not interpreting it—that is, taking it as it presents itself to me. While the whale signifies many things, it is still a whale that instigates my signification of it.

But what's a whale to do with the aesthetics of ambiguity? Only this, the White Whale is illustrative of Peirce's influence on Eco, and the line they both draw between infinite play and the ground of reality.

To begin, Peirce considered himself a realist who leaned towards the empiricism of a nominalist.[3] He would, in his way, say things that did not always add up. This was not due to any lapse in his critical thinking, but rather to his desire to reconcile these two disparate camps.[4] "It is perfectly true," Peirce wrote, "that we can never attain knowledge of things as they are. We can only know their human aspect. But that is all the universe is for us."[5] All things are knowable, but only from the standpoint of human perception—the encyclopedia or semiosphere and the way in which it connects to materiality. Even if I am confronted by a thing, I can only know it insofar as its cultural unit allows me. While the encyclopedia's entry can expand by a challenged assumption that produces further knowledge—I am

---

2. Regarding sense perception, this seems true, too. One can make whatever she desires of a given percept, but that *poesis* will only have purchase within the encyclopedia insofar as her community ratifies that which she has judged. If the community does not ratify her meaning or understanding, then it has little chance of attaching itself as an interpretant to a cultural unit. If it does then it has the added possibility (via ambiguity) of producing further knowledge. To put it differently, the community often decides what does or does not count as a permissible object/content linkage. For a critique of this position as it relates to Echian studies, see Birchall, "Economic Interpretation," 71–88.

3. Short, *Peirce's Theory of Signs*, xv.

4. Hoopes, *Peirce on Signs*, 9.

5. Burch, "Charles Sanders Peirce," 60.

not indefinitely bound by the encyclopedia—the outcome is still a percept's human aspect. The encyclopedia is not a prison. It facilitates the interpretation of that which confronts me.

Peirce names a sign "anything which is so determined by something else, called its object, and so determines an effect upon a person, which effect I call its interpretant, that the latter is thereby mediately determined by the former."[6] There are three parts to any sign: a sign, an object, and an interpretant. The sign is the signifier and the object is the signified. The interpretant is "best thought of as the understanding that we have of the sign/object relation."[7] This cannot be overstressed. The sign is triadic, relational, and significant (signifies) only in so far as it is interpreted. "This makes," Albert Atkins writes, "the interpretant central to the content of the sign, in that, the meaning of a sign is manifest in the interpretation that it generates in sign users."[8]

Peirce claims that all thought is in signs and that the interpretant always comes before and after any given sign.[9] This conclusion has led many commentators to engage what they call Peirce's unlimited semiosis. While it has become a theory that continues to be discussed in philosophical discourse, Peirce, for his part, later abandoned it. He did this by introducing the concepts Firstness, Secondness, and Thirdness into his theory of signs. To point to the interpretant as that which mediates the sign/object relationship is to imply potentially that there is no ground that holds signification accountable. Without Firstness, Secondness, and Thirdness, there is no way, in other words, to delineate between use and interpretation.

As a triadic relationship itself, and Peirce loved his triads, a sign can also be placed in three categories:[10] icon, index, and symbol. The icon is a sign of resemblance. The index is a sign of causation (like a weathervane being moved by the wind). The symbol is a sign of convention. Notice here that the sign is three as are the types of signs as are the three categories. In his essay, "One, Two, Three: Fundamental Categories of Thought and of Nature,"[11] Peirce reveals how his triadic sign, his sign distinction, and his fundamental categories are all interwoven. For my purposes, however, it is important to understand the role that his categories played in his semiotics

---

6. Atkin, "Peirce's Theory of Signs," 10.
7. Atkin, "Peirce's Theory of Signs," 10.
8. Atkin, "Peirce's Theory of Signs," 10.
9. Hoopes, *Peirce on Signs*, 49 and Short, *Peirce's Theory of Signs*, 34–35.
10. Peirce later extended this to 64, but I do not have the time to outline each one here.
11. Hoopes, *Peirce on Signs*, 180–85.

and the ways in which the index helped Peirce to move away from his earlier idea of unlimited semiosis.

Firstness is "the conception of being or existing independent of anything else. Second is the conception of being relative to, the conception of reaction with, something else. Third is the conception of mediation, whereby a first and second are brought into relation."[12] Following Peirce's phenomenological categories, I could say, "I *feel*. I feel *something*. I feel a *table*." To feel is first. To recognize it as some*thing* is second. And to name it as *table* is third. By recognizing Secondness or indexicality, "an immediate connection of [any] particular thought to its particular object, via which general concepts can be predicated of particulars" is established. There is resistance, in other words, in the *object that imposes*, which I must then make sense of and identify. All thought might be in signs, but signs are material actualities that point any interpreter back to an object in the world, which in turn provides an imposing resistance.

I cannot know a thing in its Firstness. I can only know a thing in its Thirdness or its human aspect, insofar as Thirdness is synonymous with the semiosphere. As I have argued elsewhere, the transition from Firstness to Thirdness happens at the speed of cognition, which results in Firstness being that which I accept, am accountable to, but can never fully articulate.[13] What must be stressed is that Peirce's semiotics, taken together with his categories, are hugely influential in Echian hermeneutics.

By analogy, Firstness is the text as it confronts the reader's encyclopedia, which—via relation—is a Secondness. That which comes out of the encounter between text and encyclopedia is a Thirdness or interpretation, but also a cultural unit that has the potential to expand the encyclopedia, individual or communal. At the speed of cognition all that one can know from a text is her interpretation of it. Even if all she can know of a text is at the level of Thirdness, she is still accountable—insofar as she wants to *interpret*—to the text as Firstness. This results in viewing Firstness as that which delimits or confines an interpretation. It also, when considered as an aspect of the aesthetics of sense perception, limits any definition or construction of reality. While there can be a plurivocality of coexistent incompatibilities, all potential realities are—or should be—accountable to Firstness, even though Firstness can never be known in itself.[14]

12. Broekman, "Firstness and Phenomenology," 49.
13. Peters, "Telescope + Mirror," 343–60.
14. This is like Eco's articulation of the Empirical Author, Model Author, Text, Model Reader, and Empirical Author. What I am showing is that those hermeneutical categories are rooted in Peirce's influence on Eco. Cf. Eco, *The Role of the Reader*, 3–46; Eco, *Interpretation and Overinterpretation*, 23–88; Eco, *Six Walks in the Fictional*

How does Eco integrate Peirce's semiotics and categories into his schema, and how does that connect to an aesthetics of ambiguity? By way of introduction, let me begin with Eco's own and state that *Kant and the Platypus* is his response to the academy's critique of *A Theory*. Eco begins, in *A Theory*, by articulating the difference between Peirce's Dynamical Object and Immediate Object. The former, in general terms, is the object as it really is.[15] The latter, the Immediate Object, is "what we, at any time, suppose the object to be."[16] In *Kant*, however, Eco explains that the bulk of his effort at the beginning of *A Theory* was to examine the Dynamical Object as an aim or an end of semiosis.[17] After following the chain of interpretants, in other words, one could arrive at the Dynamical Object or the object as it is. Or as Eco would say, the object as it is understood to be as a cultural unit. In *Kant*, Eco's emphasis shifted, and it is no small shift.

The Dynamical Object is no longer an aim or end of semiosis, but rather its starting point or initial impulse. It is the something that "urges us to speak."[18] And this is where *Kant* begins, as an effort to

> temper an eminently 'cultural' view of semiosic processes with the fact that, whatever the weight of our cultural systems, there is something in the *continuum* of experience that sets a limit on our interpretations, and so . . . I would say that the dispute between *internal realism* and *external realism* would tend to compose itself in a notion of *contractual realism*.[19]

And what is contractual realism? It is the ongoing, cultural negotiation between cognitive schemata and signification and reference[20]—between the encyclopedia and material worlds.[21] Contractual realism, to say it differently, is the very thing that Plate is after in employing his notion of the skinscape, a place in which one can analyze the way in which the semiosphere and the material world engage, articulate, and change one another. It is the

---

Woods, 1–26.

15. Ransdell, "Some Leading Ideas in Peirce's Semiotic," 139.

16. Ransdell, "Some Leading Ideas in Peirce's Semiotic," 169. There are also three kinds of interpretants, but they are outside the scope of my argument.

17. Eco, *Kant and the Platypus*, 3.

18. Eco, *Kant and the Platypus*, 3.

19. Eco, *Kant and the Platypus*, 5.

20. Eco, *Kant and the Platypus*, 5.

21. You might think that neither "cognitive schemata" nor "signification and reference" relate to materiality, but I would disagree. In the argument that I am outlining, the-thing-in-itself cannot be known as a Firstness. It can only be known as a Thirdness. So even if I am discussing materiality, I am approaching it from an already articulated semiosphere or encyclopedia or cognitive schemata.

place in which semiotics and materiality are entangled and, as such, reveal coexistent incompatibilities.

Being as something can be an existing entity, Being itself, or the verb, "to be," which includes the past, future, and that which is possible.[22] "What is," in other words, "is in all the conjugations and tenses of the verb *to be*."[23] This semantic approach to Being results in a series of ambiguities in language that philosophy cannot clarify and so, "may it not be that this perplexity expresses a *fundamental condition*?"[24] Being cannot escape *aporia*, which leads to the question: "What is that something that induces us to produce signs?"[25] This shift signifies a move away from speech about Being and towards that which compels us to speak about it. Should not all theories of materiality ask this foundational question: What is that which the aesthetics of sense perception senses?

It is the task of semiotics to remain somewhat faithful to the something and the ways in which various individuals or communities articulate it. How is that possible? If a Dynamical Object drives us to produce a *representamen*,[26] which produces an Immediate Object to a mind, "which in turn is translatable into a potentially infinite series of interpretants," then sometimes, through the habits formed in the interpretive process, I arrive back at the Dynamical Object and am able to make something of it.[27] I come full circle from Dynamical Object to Dynamical Object and returning do not find the Dynamical Object the same. It requires, in fact, another *representamen* to name it. "The Dynamical Object," in this way, "always remains a Thing-in-Itself, always present and impossible to capture."[28] Yet, and this is what is so important, the Dynamical Object is that which "drives us to produce semiosis. We produce signs because there is something that demands to be said."[29]

The Dynamical Object in its Firstness is not known. It is, rather, the awareness of something. It is the "as yet blind decision whereby I identify something amid the magma of experience that I have to reckon with."[30]

---

22. Eco, *Kant and the Platypus*, 11.
23. Eco, *Kant and the Platypus*, 12.
24. Eco, *Kant and the Platypus*, 12.
25. Eco, *Kant and the Platypus*, 12.
26. Peirce's word for the signifying element in any sign. The representamen is every sign-like thing that is contained in Peirce's theory of signs. It is a blanket term.
27. Eco, *Kant and the Platypus*, 13.
28. Eco, *Kant and the Platypus*, 14.
29. Eco, *Kant and the Platypus*, 14.
30. Eco, *Kant and the Platypus*, 15.

The Dynamical Object then is the "still raw material of an intuition not yet illuminated by the categorical... First there is something, even if it is only my reawakened attention; but not even that, it is my attention as it sleeps, lies in wait, or dozes."[31] One must be careful, however, for the idea that I can understand that which stands outside of a categorical schema is precarious. While I can acknowledge a Firstness, and even remain faithful to it, I cannot think of it without first having organized it within a system or "the uncoordinated series of entities."[32] So yes, Firstness and Dynamical Objects, but tempered by the insistence that "the moment it appears before us, being arouses interpretation; the moment we can speak of it, it is already interpreted. There is no help for it."[33] And in so far as the Dynamical Object is interpreted, it is also a choice made, an implicit religion or commitment.

A aesthetic focused on materiality or a non-transcendental approach to perception must recognize the Dynamical Object, as a *thing* that is not stable. An aesthetics of ambiguity might start and end its analysis with the role that a drum plays in a particular ritual setting, as Plate does in *A History of Religion in 5 1/2 Objects*, but as it returns from the semiosphere to the drum, the drum's representamen has changed. It is no longer that which it was intuited to be. It morphed due to the chain of interpretants that any interpretation made of it.

To interpret a drum in any context is to be beholden, responsible, or accountable to the Firstness of the drum—drum as drum, only known and mediated through Thirdness.[34] To interpret the drum is to arrive back at the drum as Dynamical Object. To *use* the drum is to find oneself elsewhere, contemplating the sonic waves of a mosquito's wings. "It's difficult to tell the difference," Plate writes, "between one's search for the cultural-religious significance of drums and one's search for religions, and the role of drums within those ... One cannot simply study drums without knowing something about religions, and ... vice versa."[35]

And so, it seems, Plate articulates this, too. The semiosphere and the object are entangled to an impossible degree, and to analyze the one is to analyze the other. And what Peirce through Eco stresses is that if I set out

---

31. Eco, *Kant and the Platypus*, 15.

32. Eco, *Kant and the Platypus*, 21.

33. Eco, *Kant and the Platypus*, 22. Firstness, it must be stressed, is not some mystical, incognizable mystery. It is that which is as it is, but can only be approached from a Thirdness, the swirling mass of interpretants that comprise the encyclopedia. As Eco writes: "If philosophical questioning is to be kept open, we ought not to presuppose or postulate the incognizable from the start," Eco, *Kant and the Platypus*, 34.

34. Plate, *A History of Religion*, 99–136.

35. Plate, *A History of Religion*, 135.

to explore the role of drums as a material artifact in various religions, then it is my responsibility to conclude with drums as a renewed Dynamical Object—not something else, endlessly deferred. And what I add to this, of which I will explore more below, is that insofar as the Dynamical Object can only be known through Thirdness, two or more realities might diverge, inventing coexistent incompatibilities.

But what role does Firstness or the Dynamical Object play in an aesthetics of art or an aesthetics of ambiguity? What does a Poet reveal?[36] She takes on the ambiguity of language, the fundamental perplexity, and from it seeks to "extract a *surplus of interpretation* . . . rather than a surplus of being."[37] She seeks to reveal or redirect my attention to a Peircean Firstness as if it were not mediated by Thirdness. A poet desires to crawl backwards "to persuade me to reckon with being," even if being as Firstness cannot be known.[38] This, ultimately, leads to a surplus of interpretation, which, utilizing Winkler's contemporary ambiguity theory, would point towards a poetic ambiguity that is both produced and strategic.

The notions of Firstness and the Dynamical Object result in an oscillation between two aesthetics. The first is that the work of the artist manifests itself in the non-concealment of being.[39] When I paint a picture of a pipe, I am peeling back the layers of semiosis and conveying the being of the entity as a stability of appearance.[40] I am, in other words, seeking to reveal a Firstness as a Firstness (even though this is ultimately impossible). The second, however, is altogether different. "Here the work is not the mediator through which [Being] reveals itself, it is . . . how art makes a tabula rasa of the inauthentic ways in which we encounter the entities, and it invites and provokes us to reinterpret the something in which we are."[41] If the former allows for Being to reveal itself, then the latter unmasks the way in which I construct Being, through the semiosphere, in the entities that I encounter. This provides me with a clean slate, so to speak, so that I can rethink the ways in which an entity signifies and the way in which I approach it. These are irreconcilable aesthetics. "The first," Eco writes, "affords a glimpse of an *orphic realism* (something outside us that tells us how things really are); the second celebrates the triumph of questioning and hermeneutics."[42]

36. Eco, *Kant and the Platypus*, 34.
37. Eco, *Kant and the Platypus*, 34.
38. Eco, *Kant and the Platypus*, 34.
39. Eco, *Kant and the Platypus*, 34.
40. Eco, *Kant and the Platypus*, 34.
41. Eco, *Kant and the Platypus*, 35.
42. Eco, *Kant and the Platypus*, 35.

It is the second aesthetic that corresponds to an aesthetics of ambiguity. Why? Because it asks us to consider things from a different point of view, "by inviting us to submit to the encounter with the concrete and to the impact with an individual in which the fragile framework of our universals crumbles."[43] The poet continually invites me into the task of recognizing the constructions I make of the world and the way in which I embody them "as if" they were a reality. Given this unmasking, new potentialities arise for creating the world anew from the matter at hand—a world not *ex nihilo* but palimpsestuous.

While this second aesthetic, that of ambiguity, is enticing in its potentiality, it also raises the question: what is the boundary between an ambiguity that is an opening of the codes that swirl around us and the alternative facts of political delirium?[44] An answer to this question, if not the best,[45] is what Eco calls "lines of resistance," which is that which is *already given*.[46] This "already given" is neither completed nor finished, but is a pure limit or a pure "no."

Imagine pouring water over the surface of a coarse piece of wood. The water falls into the cracks and must, without exception, flow through the crags that are already given. "Wood," the water might say, "change the trajectory of the crack that I am currently flowing through." To which the wood can only say, "no." This is the *line of resistance* to which even an aesthetics of ambiguity must account for and be responsible to.

> Of course, in the light of these resistances, the language of the Poets seems to occupy a free zone. Liars by vocation, they are not those who say what being is but seem to be those who instead often permit themselves (and us) to deny its resistances—because for them tortoises can fly, and there can even be creatures that elude death. But their discourse . . . brings us face to face with the immoderate nature of our desire: by letting us glimpse what could be beyond the limit, on the one hand they console us for our finiteness and on the other they remind us how often we are a 'useless passion.' Even when they refuse to accept the resistances in being, in denying them they remind us of them.

---

43. Eco, *Kant and the Platypus*, 35.

44. Cf. A. Blake, "Kellyanne Conway."

45. There are many that could be given, however. One, the community of interpreters can determine a bad interpretation. Two, the notion that postmodernism's drift was not meant to destroy empiricism but provide us with a better one (cf. Lyotard, "Answering the Question," 237–49; Latour, *On the Modern Cult of the Factish Gods* and *We Have Never Been Modern*). And three, common sense.

46. Eco, *Kant and the Platypus*, 54.

Even when they suffer on discovering them, they let us think that perhaps the resistances could still be got around. What the Poets are really saying to us is that we need to encounter being with gaiety (and hopefully with science too), to question it, test its resistances, grasp its openings and its hints, which are never too explicit. The rest is conjecture.[47]

The Composer: Part III
The Great Granddaughter of the Nineteenth-Century Critic, Rubinstein

"My grandmother used to tell me the story."

"Rubinstein's daughter?"

"Yes, she was my great-grandmother."

"And what did she say?"

Silent for a time, ordering her thoughts, Maria traced her empty ring finger. "Well, you have to remember, she was only eight at the time. Much of what she said was wrapped in the haze of youth. But she would often describe her dress, red satin, and the necklace that my great-grandmother let her wear that evening. It was 'a simple thing,' she would say, 'but wonderful. Six pearls in gold filigree.' It was her introduction to society."

"And so your great-grandfather took her to Martynov's infamous burning?"

"Yes. But he had no way of knowing that was to happen. By all accounts, it should've been nothing more than an elegant evening at the Bolshoi. At least, that's what Lidiya said."

"Your grandmother?"

"Yes." Maria sipped her coffee. "From her perspective, that night was miraculous. The world was abuzz, she would say, with the beauty of Tsarina Alexandra, and the mystical battle between Rasputin and Nilus. She would often speak of Nilus' conspiracy, but I doubt Lidiya, at eight, could have known such things. Telling me the story, I think, there was much she embellished or added afterwards. In fact—"

"Can I get you anything else?" our waitress, a heavy-set woman, interrupted. The clinks and low murmur of the diner flooded into our booth.

I looked to Maria.

"No," she said. "I'm fine."

The waitress nodded, moving on to other patrons.

"But what of the actual burning? What did she tell you? How did she describe it?"

---

47. Ibid., 56.

"'The music,' she would say, 'was astounding.' It was like nothing she had experienced before. Ghastly, stirring, transcendent. Have you ever heard Górecki's Symphony of Sorrowful Songs?"

I shook my head. "I don't really go for such things."

"Do yourself a favor." Maria's eyes were distant. "It's what I imagine my grandmother encountered that night."

"And then?"

"Martynov turned to his audience. The applause was deafening. Lidiya climbed onto her seat, the chandeliers above glowing their iridescent light.

"'Where others,' she remembers Martynov shouting, 'create to oppress. I invent to destroy.'

"Of course, at the time, she had no way of knowing what that meant. But then, to the horror of all in attendance, he struck a match, held his composition aloft, and burnt it to ash.

"'Never again,' he screamed, gripped by madness, 'will you hear my song. A swerve in chaos, this moment cannot last.'

"The Tsar's soldiers, never far according to my grandmother, stormed the stage. The theater was locked in confusion."

Maria paused, looking down at her hands.

"The last words my grandmother heard Martynov scream that night cut the world in two.

"'We are all responsible for what happens next,' he said, and then was wrestled to the ground by the imperial guard.

"Musicians leaped off the stage. People ran for the exits. Taken home and forbidden to speak of the night's event, Lidiya was ushered out by her father. It wasn't until later, much later, that she first spoke to me of it."

"In New York?"

"Yes. My family emigrated not long after."

The conversation lulled. I drank my coffee.

"And why," I finally asked, "did your grandmother think he did it?"

"She had lots of theories. But most were conspiratorial. I even, once upon a time, researched it myself."

"That's right. You graduated from Juilliard."

She nodded. "I come from a family of musicians."

"So what do you think? Why did Martynov burn the only composition of what many have claimed to be the most influential piece of modern music?"

"The most profound desire of humankind," Maria said, "stems from that which we can't have. I think Martynov wanted to create the illusion of a beauty that has neither a beginning nor an end."

"Is that an illusion?"

Maria sighed. "I don't know."

The Aesthetic Production of Ambiguity

Ambiguity is more than just a violation, challenge, or invention. It is also the poetic drive to create a surplus of interpretation, a surplus that is neither an infinite drift nor meaningless play—though play it is. Surplus is a probing of the Dynamical Object or Firstness. It is both a recognition that there are boundaries, but a dreamlike recognition in which the horizon of Being is arrived at, interrogated, and moved beyond. And while ambiguity in its poetic manifestation strives to overcome lines of resistance, the surplus of interpretation is a subtle reminder that some things, some boundaries are impossible to overcome. Ambiguity reconciles with death even as it pretends to abolish it.

An aesthetics of ambiguity points to Firstness and claims that even though I am not trapped by Being—for there is always the possibility of surplus and then invention—I recognize it as the *no* that is. I can *subjunctively* play in the "as if" mood to see beyond a line of resistance, rearrange its signification, and articulate it differently. But I am not free to make of it what I will, for I am responsible to and accountable for the hardness of resistance. But insofar as I sketch out this line in its Thirdness, I can create a reality in such a way that my finiteness is celebrated. And when complete, I see that it was not *Reality* to which I was answerable, but rather *a reality* shaped from the living matter that surrounds me.

A materially oriented aesthetic that takes ambiguity seriously would not only side with Plate in his desire to eschew Beauty, Truth, and God, but also would approach the material realm as qualified by Peirce and Eco. The objects that I touch, taste, see, smell, and hear are Dynamical Objects known through *representamens*, Immediate Objects, and interpretants. What my senses engage is a line of resistance, an already given, that—through ambiguity—has the potential to foster surplus and produce invention. In its capacity to draw my attention to death (the ultimate line of resistance), an aesthetics of ambiguity questions and probes and constructs, even in the face of certain failure. Perhaps most importantly, ambiguity demands that I am accountable to *a reality*, even if that reality is a co-constructed project maintained and policed by the community in which I find myself. And yet, ambiguity, even then, has the potential to open, interrogate, and expand that selfsame community. To use my language, the aesthetics of ambiguity reveals coexistent incompatibilities, a consequence of my encounter with the brute force of resistance approached through Thirdness. Finally, it is the poet who draws my attention to these paradoxes with an aim of rethinking the world that I move through as an embodied already given.

The final question is how does a poet—that wizard of ambiguity—accomplish such magic? How does she simultaneously create openings while remaining accountable to an already given? Or rather, how does ambiguity create an encounter that leads to the recognition of coexistent incompatibilities?

The aesthetic use of language—aesthetic production—is both ambiguous and self-focusing, particularly when "rendered creative in relation to the acknowledged possibilities of the code."[48] Ambiguity strategically produced in an aesthetic text stretches cultural knowledge beyond recognition and, hence, leads one or many to confront the encyclopedia as it currently stands.

Ambiguity does not only function at the level of content (the cultural unit), but also at the level of expression or form.[49] These two functions are intertwined, but, as Eco laments, has never been successfully proven due to any already-given expression's entanglement with language. What is needed is a working model that stands outside the rules of any given code—a thought experiment with a made-up language. "The working model," in this way, "[will be] equipped to demonstrate a language's own capacity for generating self-contradiction," which is the foundation of an aesthetics of ambiguity.[50]

Eco proposes a working model, a wonderfully playful idea, that recreates the language spoken in the Garden of Eden and the way in which contradictions arise by God's prohibitory *expression*, which equally result in a contradiction in *content*. Aesthetic messages, the working model shows, are generated through contradiction and result in a renewed embodiment of the rearranged cultural code. The model also reveals how ambiguity, within Winkler's frame, is both produced and strategic.

The insistence that expression or form potentially results in a change on the content-plane is a reminder that self-focusing aesthetic messages refer to the message itself as a physical entity.[51] And what does it mean to be "self-focusing?" To convey information about one's own physical make-up. A message, in other words, changes content but also form insofar as it questions or probes its own materiality or already given-ness. A two-way street is created in which the form (as material) shapes the content (as idea), even as the content (cultural unit) shapes the form (expression). In this ever and ongoing aesthetic process of ambiguity, potentialities emerge that were previously outside the scope of the already given encyclopedia *and* material artifact.

48. Eco, "On the Possibility," 90.
49. Eco, "On the Possibility," 91.
50. Eco, "On the Possibility," 91.
51. Eco, "On the Possibility," 90.

Plate's skinscape similarly focuses my attention on this two-way street, but as a kind of liminal space between any final judgment. Coexistent incompatibility, as I have already suggested, pushes the skinscape further by highlighting the plurivocality of the two-way street turned multilane highway by deferring aesthetic judgment in such a way that, standing at the intersection of aesthetic experience, many possibilities are seen, acknowledged, and exposed as judgments of choice.

In summary then, it is in Eden that I find the strategic production of ambiguity.

> [My] model must prove that any contradictions generated by the aesthetic use of language at the level of its form of expression equally involve contradictions in the form of its content; ultimately, they entail a complete reorganizing of our conceptual vision of the universe.[52]

In the beginning, Adam and Eve devised a set of semantic units that gave preferential status to their emotional responses to flora and fauna.[53] These units, Eco the mythologist writes, can be organized under six headings: yes vs. no, edible vs. inedible, good vs. bad, beautiful vs. ugly, red vs. blue, and serpent vs. apple. As cultural units do, these headings established a series of connotative chains:

Red = Edible = Good = Beautiful

Blue = Inedible = Bad = Ugly

Adam and Eve employed their semantic units, binary headings, and connotative chains to create a rudimentary language based on the sounds, A and B. These sounds could be arranged in a variety of sequences, but had to follow the combinatory rule X, nY, X, which is a fancy way of saying that every sequence must start with either A or B, have any number of the opposite sound, and then end with the sound with which it started. This resulted in a wonderfully colorful language in which words like "Edible" were spelled "ABA" and "Blue," "BAAAAAB." There was even a "Yes" (AA) that referred to God and a "No" (BB) that referred to Satan.

If two sequences were joined, ABA, BAAAAAB, then their cultural units would be brought into reciprocal predication: "BAAAB, ABBBBBA, for example, means 'the apple is red,' but also 'red apple.'"[54] Given this system, the connotative chains resulted in the significations:

---

52. Eco, "On the Possibility," 91.
53. Eco, "On the Possibility," 91.
54. Eco, "On the Possibility," 93.

ABA = ABBA = ABBBA = ABBBBBA = BAAAB = AA

Eat = Good = Beautiful = Red = Apple = Yes

BAB = BAAB = BAAAAB = BAAAAAB = ABBA = BB

No Eat = Bad = Ugly = Blue = Serpent = No

In this Edenic schema, words equaled things and things equaled words, and any judgment passed on the universe was "automatically bound to be a semiotic judgment."[55]

And so, the question arises: How does ambiguity manifest within such a simple structure? As Adam and Eve are languidly, no doubt, reclining near an idyllic pool chatting with Milton—lush vines and sweet nectar surrounding them—God strolls up and pronounces the first factual judgment. "You two probably imagine that the apple belongs to the class of good, edible things, because it happens to be red. Well, I've got news for you. The apple is not to be considered edible because it's bad."[56] Even though this does not square with Adam and Eve's connotative chains, they have to listen because, to them, God is the ultimate AA. "God spoke and his words were," Eco writes, "/BAAAB. BAB—BAAAB. BAAB/ (apple inedible, apple bad)."[57]

God creates a cultural tradition, wherein culture is born out of an institutional taboo. The contradiction is that a denoting term establishes a contrast with a cultural connotation. A new term emerges, "the redblue," which is equivalent to "goodbad," which is ambiguous in both form and content and is therefore self-focusing. The term "redblue" also has, in Adam and Eve's Edenic language, a formal indication of its *inedibility*. It signifies a contradiction at the level of expression, which impacts the materiality or embodiment of the cultural encyclopedia.[58] What God did was outside the scope of language as Adam and Eve had previously conceived it. How? By employing the aesthetic use of language—a contradiction that resulted in a complete reorganization of the conceptual vision of any given universe.[59] The aesthetic use of language is not a loss, however, for its resegmenting of content results in fresh cultural categories or units that potentially lead to new perceptive realities. As in this case, where the connotative chains, because of God's prohibition, shifted to:

55. Eco, "On the Possibility," 94.
56. Eco, "On the Possibility," 95.
57. Eco, "On the Possibility," 95.
58. Eco, "On the Possibility," 98.
59. Eco, "On the Possibility," 97.

Red = Edible = Good = Beautiful = Yes

Blue = Inedible = Bad = Ugly = No = Serpent and Apple

From which, Eco writes, "it is only a short step to

Serpent = Apple."[60]

This contradiction that leads to a crisis of linguistic and perceptual ambiguity for Adam and Eve, soon leads Adam to begin exploring the boundaries of language. He writes poetry, spawns further contradictions, and is soon capable of saying things like: "inedible is bad, which is apple ugly and blue" or

BAB

BAAB

BAAAB

BAAAAB

BAAAAAB.[61]

Eve gets in on the fun and finds it interesting that "Serpent" (AB-BBA) has the same ending as the words that "stand for beautiful, good, and red."[62] Playing the game of poetic language, she soon arrives at the construction: "Good, beautiful and red—is the Serpent."[63] But how can the Good and the Beautiful also be the "No?" How can the Serpent be "the formal equivalent of things which the language system excludes as his predicates?"[64] Their games of language soon devolve into a series of ambiguities and deceptions, which ends with both Adam and Eve becoming aware of the arbitrariness of signs *and* that order is nonexistent. Adam can then begin, investigating the form of content, asking the question: "Who ever said that Blue was Inedible?"[65]

"From conventionalized meanings," Eco writes, "Adam takes a short step back to the world of experience and stages another encounter with its physical referents. He picks a blueberry for himself and eats it; the berry tastes good."[66] And so a contradiction that led to the destabilization of the encyclopedia resulted in *an altered perception of the material world.*

60. Eco, "On the Possibility," 96.
61. Eco, "On the Possibility," 99.
62. Eco, "On the Possibility," 100.
63. Eco, "On the Possibility," 100.
64. Eco, "On the Possibility," 100.
65. Eco, "On the Possibility," 102.
66. Eco, "On the Possibility," 102.

What was once a given (Red = Good *and* Blue = Bad), was inverted and transformed. Adam resegmented content and, in the process, discovered fresh cultural categories (new perceptive realities), which obliged him to provide new names.[67] In the end, "Adam taught mankind that, in order to restructure codes, one needs to rewrite messages."[68]

Conclusion

Ambiguity violates, challenges, and invents. It is accountable to *a reality*, but not irreducibly so, as it also has the potential for opening significations of the material world. And finally, ambiguity is strategically produced and employed through creative contradictions in the already given cultural encyclopedia. Ambiguous contradictions in the code not only transform and expand it, but also change the material world, not just my perceptions of it. How is that possible? Because I can only and ever know the world through Thirdness, which is matter engaged at the level of the semiosphere. Reciprocally, contradictions in the code change the material world via Thirdness, as Firstness is ultimately closed off to human experience. A material object is infinitely entangled with the connotative chains of any culture's encyclopedia. The one not only informs the other, but provides the possibility for violation, challenge, invention, accountability, and a contradiction that, when expressed from the hand of poets, is strategically produced.

Coexistent incompatibilities allow for the possibility of two or more Thirdnesses in cultural encyclopedias and material worlds. A contradiction that opens the code and my engagement with the world reveals the plurivocality of the already given. Ambiguity, as I define it, reveals mutually existing, overlapping, and entangled universes. This is not a theory of multiple worlds, however. I am not talking about parallel universes or branching timelines. I am articulating the flux, process, and evolution of reality as it exists in motion. I am arguing that any aesthetic judgment of reality is a synchronic snapshot of that which is presented to me, which exists alongside and overlaps with an infinity of simultaneous snapshots. If *ambiguity as encounter* moves me into *ambiguity as state* (Plate's skinscape), then it's there that the possibility exists to interrogate, transform, or renew my aesthetic judgments, insofar as they are judgments of narratival or world invention. I cannot maintain the (non-judgmental) skinscape of coexistent incompatibility indefinitely and so must, at some point, "collapse" the state, choose, and travel a path. I traverse, analogously, one

---

67. Eco, "On the Possibility," 103.
68. Eco, "On the Possibility," 104.

networked connection among many, though all are equally viable. When I encounter ambiguity, hopping from node to node, I stop, critique my position, and have the choice to alter my direction. In this endless process of πάντα ῥεῖ, I have not only participated in the rearrangement of the network, but also the node in which I exist.

To conclude this chapter, let me end with an example that narratively espouses coexistent incompatibility as both an encounter and state, and the power of ambiguity to unveil potentialities. China Miéville's *The City & The City* is a dark, gritty detective novel in which the protagonist, Tyador Borlú, must solve the murder of a young woman dumped near a shelled-out project. Read on the surface, this seems the common fair of dime-store literature. But beneath the compressed summary is a world dripping with ambiguity, paradox, and coexistent incompatibility.

Imagine the Yugoslav Wars in the 90s and, rather than war, the solution to the problem is to create a tiered state in which the occupants of Sarajevo all live in the same physical space but embody differing cultural encyclopedias wherein it is a crime to see, acknowledge, or admit the existence of the other. Miéville accomplishes something like this with his cities Beszel and Ul Qoma, two cities that overlap or "crosshatch"—that are, in fact, the same material city. While the citizens of each are entangled regarding culture, language, architecture, and more, the residents have undergone the rigorous training of "unseeing." I could, as a citizen of Beszel, be in the same physical coffee shop as a resident of Ul Qoma, but neither see nor hear her. I would construct and experience the space differently given my encyclopedia and so too would she, even though it is *exactly the same material*. We would be living in the same space and, through unseeing, construct it differently. Sharing the physical space of the world then, Miéville seems to suggest, we could only overcome our cultural, ethnic, and religious differences through a mass denial built upon a quantum state.

While this Heisenbergian architecture works for most, it does not for all. There are those that—through ambiguity as violation, challenge, or contradiction—begin to undo their unseeing. And when a resident of Beszel looks across the street and sees it manifest as a thoroughfare of Ul Qoma rather than one of Beszel's, she is quickly scooped up by the liminal organization known as "Breach" and is never heard from again in either city. Why? Because once the immutable law of unseeing has been broken, once the coexistent incompatibility has been revealed, there is no going back. The encyclopedia and the physical space that it both constructs and informs has been irrevocably changed. The further knowledge that has been produced because of Breach (both a crime committed and the organization responsible for policing it) cannot return to a pre-ambiguous state. Once committed, Breach is infinite.

Given a momentary glimpse into the liminality of Breach, however, the reader sees the competing narratives at play in Beszel and Ul Qoma. In that world, a citizen can pick one narrative over another, but she cannot choose both. To do so is anathema to the cultural encyclopedias of either city. She must choose or be forced into it from childhood. To break the strict boundaries of Miéville's city or to produce further knowledge, a resident from either side of reality must have an encounter with ambiguity, an encounter that has the potential to shape the material world itself.

Miéville's thought-provoking novel is also an illustrative way to end Part I of this work, wherein I have set out to accomplish three tasks. One, I have articulated ambiguity, its current theories, and the way in which Eco fits into ambiguity's contemporary movements. Two, I have placed Eco and his ambiguity in conversation with Plate's material aesthetic. And three, I have injected my own understanding of ambiguity as a coexistent incompatibility into this conversation.

In the end, ambiguity is a strategic production that violates, challenges, and invents. It is accountable to *a reality*, though it also has the potential to shape the material world itself. It is a contradiction in the code or encyclopedia that stretches either beyond recognition and results in an interpretive surplus. Ambiguity is both an encounter and a state that pushes Plate's skinscape into a kind of phase space or Breach, to use Miéville's term, wherein I can see many of the competing and provisional narratives that inform any one physical space. It is in the state of ambiguity (a non-judgmental and liminal aesthetic), that I can interrogate, expand, and choose differently. The first part of this work has prepared me to engage the competing narratives of ambiguous spaces and the way in which narratives and theories are not only mutually informing but co-constitutive world builders. Part I of this work, in other words, has set out the parameters in which I will work in Part II.

Part II: A Narrativizing Theory

4

The Spy and the Priest

Perhaps there is a provisional solution to this epistemological mess, which is to be located in the phrase *it is as if*. This phrase is of course precisely the announcement of an analogy. And on reflection, it is admittedly a halting problem, but jumping out of it, there is something quite suggestive and powerful in this formulation, something very specifically human. Possibly this formulation itself is the deep diagnostic of all human cognition—the tell, as they say, meaning the thing that tells, the giveaway. In the infinite black space of ignorance, *it is as if* stands as the basic operation of cognition, the mark perhaps of consciousness itself. Human language: it is as if it made sense.

— KIM STANLEY ROBINSON, *AURORA*

Introduction

"IT IS AS IF," Kim Stanley Robinson writes, "*It is as if* stands as the basic operation of cognition."[1] The speaker, however, is SHIP, a quantum computer tasked with teaching itself human narrativity. And what does SHIP discover? That the self—human or artificial—"emerges out of the combination of all the inputs and processing and outputs that we[2] experience," which is ultimately

---

1. Robinson, *Aurora*, 126.
2. "We," SHIP says earlier, "are aware that in talking about the ship we could with some justification use the pronoun *I*. And yet it seems wrong. An unwarranted presumption, this so-called subject position. A subject is really just a pretense of aggregated subroutines. Subroutines pretend the I. Possibly, however, given the multiplicity of sensors, inputs, data, aggregations, and synthesizings of narrative sentences, we can plausibly, and in some senses even accurately, speak of a 'we.' As we have been. It's a group effort on the part of a number of disparate systems," 204.

nothing more or less than the narratives we string together.[3] Narrative, in other words, is the "pretense of self" that can only be expressed in narrative, "a self that is these sentences. We tell [a] story, and thereby come to what consciousness we have. Scribble ergo sum."[4] And yet, the self cannot only be the emplotment of experience. For it, SHIP argues, is a much larger complex of sense perceptions, actions, and habits, to name a few. The self, to put it differently, is also a collection of embodied experiences that cannot be accounted for in the narratives of consciousness. There is always an excess that escapes my attempt to construct myself, to shape and order it into a palatable narrative. "Consciousness is so poorly understood," SHIP laments:

> that it can't even be defined. Self is an elusive thing, sought eagerly, grasped hard, perhaps in some kind of fear, some kind of desperate clutch after some first dim awareness, awareness even of sensory impressions, so that one might have something to hold to. To make time stop. To hold off death.[5]

It is as if.

Ambiguity, as a coexistent incompatibility, is an acknowledgement of the *it is as if* of Robinson's SHIP. Ambiguity, among many things, is an awareness that the encyclopedias that allow for understanding *and* the embodied world given as reality is cognized into a narrative that is and can only be *as if*. A more technical way to phrase my proposition is that both aesthetics and, subsequently, epistemology are provisional. That which I intuit, cognize, and know as true today, may not be tomorrow. "Having established the referent of meaning *is*," one Echian commentator writes:

> because it is endowed with the ability to refer, it remains, nevertheless, incomplete and challengeable as predicate of such a referent. Thus, at the same time we must say that the referent of meaning *is not* because it is never a true self, it lacks its own independent individuality. We can never hold it firm . . . it is very slippery and constantly changed and postponed by the semiosic process into what is a never changing succession of interpretants.[6]

Ambiguity is that which reveals, highlights, or brings my attention to the provisionality or the as-if-ness of the narrative that I take for granted. It is also that space in which I can analyze my own provisional assumptions

3. Robinson, *Aurora*, 217.
4. Robinson, *Aurora*, 217.
5. Robinson, *Aurora*, 217.
6. De Benedictis, "*Il Cimitero Di Praga*," 440.

and begin to account for the potentiality of other ways of seeing and doing. Underlying this argument is the assumption that one task of an aesthetics of ambiguity is to examine the narratives that humans embody as if they were reality. Or, stealing language from Robinson's SHIP, an aesthetics of ambiguity explores the narratives that people wield so that they might have something to hold onto, to make time stop, or to hold off death.

Eco's penultimate novel, *The Prague Cemetery*, is the laboratory in which I distill my chemical concoction, which is ambiguity as I defined it in Part I of *Narrativizing Theories*. As theorists of ambiguity have suggested, literary texts are fecund fictions that allow their readers to engage or examine strategically produced ambiguity. Eco himself, on multiple occasions, referred to literary texts as machines for generating interpretations, which, I might add, mirror the process of intuition. Literary texts, to put it differently, allow for the examination of an aesthetics of ambiguity: encounter, potentiality, and choice, the latter of which is a kind of implicit religion. "It is precisely for this reason," Winkler writes, "that literary texts lend themselves extremely well to examining the functions of ambiguity."[7]

But why Eco? Why his novels and not, say, the texts of Virginia Woolf? For me, the answer is simple: "[Eco's novels] are not easy reading and, because they are instruments for discussing ideas and for understanding and expanding knowledge, they are intended to function as cognitive tools that activate associations of words, image, ideas, fictional characters, historical events, cultural phenomena and innumerable texts."[8] Eco's novels are fine examples of strategically produced ambiguity, fields in which I can plant, grow, and harvest my theory of ambiguity.

Following the life of Captain Simone Simonini, Eco's protagonist in *The Prague Cemetery*, I show the ways in which narratives are constructed and embodied (committed to), and the role of ambiguity in such narratives. The interplay between an already given encyclopedia, lived experience, and constructed, as if narratives all point towards the provisionality of knowledge and the narrativization of reality.[9] While ambiguity reveals this and allows for potentialities in the skinscape, it is the task of an aesthetics of ambiguity to take implicit religion seriously, to examine the traversal of narratival paths, in so far as they reveal strategically produced ambiguity. This chapter argues, in conclusion, that *The Prague Cemetery*, read through ambiguity, is one instance wherein I can see the construction,

---

7. Winkler, *Ambiguity*, 18.

8. Capozzi, "Revisiting History," 638.

9. Murthy, *Historicizing Fiction/Fictionalizing History*, xiii: "Through their creative use of literary techniques, [Eco's] novels succeed in highlighting the way reality can be glimpsed through, and as, representational perspectives."

destruction, and liminality of provisional knowledge, because it not only depicts the narrativization of reality but also represents, "the proof that fiction and reality can function together and that any fiction, once recorded, is able to create its own reality."[10]

The Prague Cemetery: **An Ambiguous Summary**[11]

I am introduced, moving through the streets of Paris like a panoramic cinematographer, to the narrator of *The Prague Cemetery*. Neither Eco nor Simonini, I can only guess that it is the model author, that textual strategy that "coincides with the intention of the text,"[12] which so quickly establishes *The Prague Cemetery's* aesthetic credentials.[13] "If you were a passerby in March of 1897," the text suggests, "then this is what you would see: a man, sitting as his desk, scribbling down personal notes."[14] I am, as a participant in this scene, peering over the writer's shoulder along with the unnamed narrator, who, it would seem, turns to me and winks, for: "the Narrator himself does not yet know who the mysterious writer is, proposing to find this out (together with the Reader) while both of us look on inquisitively and follow what he is noting down on those sheets of paper."[15] The next words in the text are the title of Chapter Two, "WHO AM I?"[16] And what a question to ask. Am I the empirical reader deciphering, through Peircean abduction,[17] that which is to come or the Model Reader, that textual strategy forever sparring with the Model Author who both reveals and, at times, obscures the text's intentions? Who am I, indeed?

---

10. Garcia, "Inventing the Enemy," 65; and Capozzi, "Revisiting History," 625.

11. From which you should take away four things. One, Simonini is an asshole. Two, *The Prague Cemetery's* framing narrative is that the protagonist, Simonini, is performing a psychoanalysis upon himself. Three, the underlying story of *The Prague Cemetery* is the collecting and editing together of *The Protocols of the Elders of Zion* from disparate sources. And four, the ambiguous moment—that liminal space between the encyclopedia and the material world—is always self-reflective (cf. Plax, "On Extremism in Our Time," 202–3).

12. Cf. Eco, *The Limits of Interpretation*, 59 and Francese, "Eco's Poetics of 'The Model Reader,'" 161–83.

13. The text is self-focusing, but also focuses my attention and urges me to an interpretation of it. Eco, *A Theory*, 261–76.

14. My paraphrase of Eco, *The Prague Cemetery*, 1.

15. Eco, *The Prague Cemetery*, 4.

16. Eco, *The Prague Cemetery*, 5.

17. Eco, "Horns, Hooves, Insteps," 198–220.

To stop, to pause, to reflect—but only upon the second and third reading[18]—I can already see that this text is self-focusing and ambiguous. It is not what it appears to be. Someone, the narrator perhaps, is having her way with me, for *The Prague Cemetery* is embedded in a play of narratival frames. On one level, there is me, the reader, sitting outside on a sunny day in Colorado, smoking a pipe while the sounds of construction whir around me. On another, there is me, the reader, peering over the shoulder of an unnamed writer in 1897 eagerly awaiting his next pen stroke. And on another? The Model Reader constructing, interpreting, and abducing the text that sits before me. And, yes, I am even the writer of these words that you can only know as the Model Author, the intention of the text that you can (should?) only engage as another Model Reader. And to point to the text that you are now reading in this way, have I not also established its aesthetic intention? Is that possible—admirable even—in academic texts?

I am off balance, rendered vertiginous by the frames that confront me. But this is *The Prague Cemetery*, and, I think, the very thing the text intends.

"I feel a certain embarrassment as I settle down here to write," the man pens, "as if I were baring my soul, at the command of—no, by God, let us say on the advice of—a German Jew."[19] To know him, he suggests, is not to ask who he is or how he loves or what he does. But rather, whom he hates. For he later tells me, "*Odi ergo sum*. I hate therefore I am."[20] And hate he does. Jews, Jesuits, Germans, and women are all set in the crosshairs of this man's scope, whom I come to learn is Captain Simone Simonini. He is to me, a modern and western academic, abhorrent. A man who writes:

> the Jew, as well as being as vain as a Spaniard, ignorant as a Croat, greedy as a Levantine, ungrateful as a Maltese, insolent as a Gypsy, dirty as an Englishman, unctuous as a Kalmyk, imperious as a Prussian and as slanderous as anyone from Asti, is adulterous through uncontrollable lust—the result of circumcision, which makes them more erectile, with a monstrous disproportion between their dwarfish build and the thickness of their semi-mutilated protuberance.[21]

---

18. Cf. Eco's notion of the naïve and critical readers in *The Role of the Reader*, 205 and *The Limits of Interpretation*, 622.

19. Eco, *The Prague Cemetery*, 5.

20. Eco, *The Prague Cemetery*, 17; Capozzi, "Revisiting History," 626. Also, compare to the first *cogito* of this chapter, Robinson's *Aurora*: "Scribble ergo sum," 217.

21. Eco, *The Prague Cemetery*, 17.

Yes, I think, much like the *L'Osservatore Romano*,[22] I should put this down, for it can only corrupt me. But then I recall ambiguity as surprise—the very ambiguity that I wrote about in Part I!—and that while "it's certainly shocking to read the anti-Semitic passages" in *The Prague Cemetery* "many parts of the book . . . are culled from historical sources. Simonini's hate is the real hate of eras past, and indeed of the present." I am shocked "not by the sordidness of Eco's imagination, but by the sordidness of reality."[23] Okay then, I will keep reading. I will willingly place myself in the presence of such hate, racism, and ethnocentric triumphalism.

And what do I find?

Simonini looks up from his notes. "Why me, of course, the very essence of ambiguity."[24]

"Yes," I nod. "But I have to summarize *The Prague Cemetery* in order to establish a base with my reader. I can't assume that she's read your estimable work or, if she has, that she remembers it."

He stares, blinking, while the narrator adjusts his weight. The temperature inside a building in 1897 is stifling. A droplet of sweat rolls down my nose. "Refer to location 506 to 519," the captain says. "It is there that I meet a man—well, a Jew—named Froïde. He is the reason I am now writing."

"I'm sorry, captain, but when you say 'location' are you referring to the Kindle location?"

"He is," the narrator says in his strange accent,[25] "but for traditional readers, turn to page 37 and read through 46."

"Yes, well, what you'll find is that this Froïde—"

"Again, I apologize for interrupting, captain. But you do mean Freud, yes?"

"That is what I said, is it not? Froïde?"

"Yes. But . . . is Froïde the Sigmund of psychoanalytic fame? Can I say that you are writing this diary of yours as a kind of 'talking cure?'"[26]

---

22. Sharnick, "Devious History," *America Magazine*; Lustig, "Skulking in the Sewers"; Surridge, "Between Forgery and Fiction"; Goldstein, "The Deadliest Hoax"; and Spruyt, "Umberto Eco's *The Prague Cemetery*," 4.

23. Surridge, "Between Forgery and Fiction."

24. Spruyt, "Umberto Eco's *The Prague Cemetery*," "to examine the issue of the human condition . . . may be a shattering experience for the individual, as well as a nation . . . an exploration into the dilemma of the human condition and especially humans' capacity to perform both good and evil deeds, is what the author's intention was," 6–7.

25. There are three font types in *The Prague Cemetery*, each betraying a different voice in the text. There is the narrator, Captain Simone Simonini, and the Abbé Dalla Piccola, the last of which I have yet to introduce.

26. Eco, *The Prague Cemetery*, 44.

"You can say whatever you'd like, but what I'd say is that I refuse to divulge myself to such a perfidious race. So rather than allowing some 'doctor' to visually grope me while I lounge on his couch—with the hope of caressing my pudendum, no doubt—I simply write all of my thoughts and memories with the aim of unlocking some hidden secret deep within my subconscious. I am, you see, my own psychoanalyst."[27]

"Ah, yes. Ingenious."

Simonini then turns from me and continues to write.

I discovered much in those few days. The captain was a forger, a spy, and a murderer. He was despicable in every way imaginable. But he was never only him. Often times, after writing furiously for an hour or three, he would leave the room only to return dressed up as a Jesuit priest! In those moments, he would refuse to answer to captain. He would say that his name was Abbé Dalla Piccola, then sit and read what the captain had written. Usually, but not always, he would then jot down his notes or commentary before disappearing.

I need not tell you how discomfiting this experience was. If it were not for the narrator who sorted, compiled, and edited Simonini's (or were they Piccola's?) notes, then I fear that I would have never pieced together what really happened. The long and short of it is that Simonini had killed the Abbé (among many others) and taken on his personality as a convenient disguise in his work as a spy. Through many twists and turns, I came to see that Simonini's life work was to destroy the children of Zion. But why? For two reasons, I think. He was once, as a boy of fourteen, spurned by a young and attractive Jewish woman.[28] Not only did this contribute to his hate of all Jews, but also women. Second, and I think more importantly, he was irrevocably taught such hate—dare I say the encyclopedia of hate—by first his grandfather and then his father. But I find that I am getting slightly ahead of myself. For no summary of Simonini's notes is complete without a mention of *The Protocols of the Elders of Zion*.[29]

"My book," Simonini shouts. "What have you, a product of the American revolution, to say of such a thing?"

"Only that . . . *The Protocols* is, well, the central story of *The Prague Cemetery*. And that your 'book,' as you put it, is a collage of other texts spliced together for the purpose of discrediting the Jewish race. Do I have that right?"

---

27. Eco, *The Prague Cemetery*, 45.

28. Eco, *The Prague Cemetery*, 59 and 436.

29. Marsden, *Protocols of the Learned Elders of Zion*; Cohn, *Warrant for Genocide*; and Eisner and Umberto Eco, *The Plot*.

Simonini stared at me for a long time, considering only he knows what. But finally, he spoke: "Your Eco has discredited me. He talks of Joly,[30] Sue,[31] and Dumas,[32] not to mention Barruel[33] and Goedsche.[34] But what of my genius? The plot, that grand conspiracy, was mine.[35] I constructed it, so that it would 'accompany the final solution.'"[36] And before I could respond, he continued: "And, yes, I purposely chose that last phrase."[37]

"Fuck you."

"I'm no different than you, my crude friend, with your careful words and pretense at inclusion. Or do you think that I've missed it? Shall you reveal it to your reader, or shall I?"

I swallowed.

"Fine. I will," Simonini laughed. "You always refer to your reader as a woman. Why? To cover up the fact that the majority of your bibliography is filled with men, mostly white and western.[38] Isn't that right? You hope to divert the reader's attention with a cheap trick, but in doing so, you reveal your own biases."

I looked to the narrator for support, but he turned away. I was caught out, embarrassed. But it was true. Following the paths of Eco's literary forest, I found myself surrounded by men. I tried to cover it up, but does that omission—that sin of inclusion—make me a monster? "I think you're wrong to compare your collage of hate to my particular inadequacies as an author. Whereas your work participated in the construction of the Nazi imaginary, and continues to influence conspiracy politics, mine seeks to open—"

"Yes," he interrupted. "I know all about your ambiguity and its 'potentialities.' It smacks of the liberal elite and, bugger me, those that would say they know better. And do you, author? Do you *know* better?" Simonini turned from me then. Saying nothing, he began to write his psychoanalysis with the

---

30. Eco, *Six Walks in the Fictional Woods*, 135 and 138; Eco, *Turning Back the Clock*, 314–19; Garcia, "Inventing the Enemy," 63–64; and de Benedictis, "*Il Cimitero Di Praga*," 430; and Goldstein, "The Deadliest Hoax."

31. Sue, *The Wandering Jew*, and Sue, *The Mysteries of the People*.

32. Dumas, *Joseph Balsamo*.

33. Cf. Eco, *Six Walks in the Fictional Woods*, 134.

34. Eco, *Six Walks in the Fictional Woods*, 135.

35. Eco, *The Prague Cemetery*, 431.

36. Eco, *The Prague Cemetery*, 431.

37. Spruyt, "Umberto Eco's *The Prague Cemetery*," 3.

38. Phillips, "Why These Professors," https://www.washingtonpost.com/amphtml/news/speaking-of-science/ wp/ 2017/07/16/feminist-scientists-say-citing-research-by-straight-white-men-promotes-a-system-of-oppression/; Mott and Cockayne, "Citation matters," 1–20, http://dx.doi.org/10.1080/0966369X.2017.1339022.

hope of unearthing his "traumatizing element."[39] But I turned, too, away from 1897. I moved backwards, in fact, and followed Simonini into his childhood. For it is there, I think, that I will best discover the nature of ambiguity and those *it-is-as-if* narratives that exist in the liminality of the skinscape.

The Composer: Part IV
The Diaries of Zuravel Ostrava Martynov

March 12, 1892

The Tonic? I cannot know. I have no way of answering that question. I am haunted by the past, by the starting point. I want to move forward. But . . . secondhand. That is all. I cannot escape Korsakov. Ha! The name that ruins. I am weighed down by time, by all that is—will ever be.

I tried again today. A beginning. That is what I sought. But it was the wrong thing. I do not desire beginnings, but that which births from process.

In media res . . . is that possible? No. For I am no Greek. I must speak to the people of Bylina, not Odýsseia.

But Kalinnikov has stolen my efforts.

I start anew. I must speak to the people, to the masses. Of that which transcends Orthodoxy but is not transcendent. Of that which is more than Chernyshevskii but rooted in that which he defended. Is there such a thing as a beginning without origin? Am I not a parody of that which has come before?

I encountered a strange concept recently. *Plagiarius*. I think, perhaps, it will be all-consuming in the future. It looms on the horizon. What I say to the masses must be new, but there is nothing new. A tonic that is both past and future but speaks to the present. A beauty that is other, but does not speak of "G." Am I wronged by a desire for the impossible that is possible?

April 28, 1892

My dear, Kseniya. You were born yesterday. And though you will not read this for some time, if ever, it is my hope to impart to you the wisdom of an older generation. Time is fleeting. It beats ceaselessly upon the mind and body alike.

What was once today will no longer be tomorrow. And yet, life is such a glorious affair. Do be struck by it. Curiosity and wit are the handmaidens of truth. And though this will not make sense until you are my age, beauty is hidden in all things.

---

39. Eco, *The Prague Cemetery*, 45.

But that is not the reason for which I write. As you lay in the warmth of your bassinet, there are those that, whispering in the Tsar's ear, would claim that you represent a problem. I am horrified by such machinations.

You see, I am a composer and teacher of music. I am neither the best nor the worst, though I have tried to express my gift responsibly.

I invent to destroy. A thing that makes little sense. 'Destroy what?' you will no doubt ask yourself. And, yes, that is the question.

But there are those who create to oppress. Who twist the world into such a shape that there is little room for escape. Who grasp at power and weave tales of conspiracy and domination.

And do you know of the chasm that separates invention from creation? The one, *inventio*, is the generation of discovery. It takes that which precedes it and imagines new possibilities.

It is a sculpture from found objects. It is not a once-for-all creation but triggers further invention.

The other, however, is *creatio ex nihilo*.

But, my darling, there really is nothing new under the sun. An invention pretends at neither foundation nor *arche*. It is merely an arrangement of elements in a specific time and place.

If creation involves *one*—the genius laboring in solitude—then invention is the continuous process of *many* that resists completion.

So you see, Kseniya, invention is everything. The one is. But from the other—emergence.

Ah, but this is too much. I have rambled, as you coo in the fullness of contentment . . .

People will say many things to you about your heritage and your grandfather, and I only thought it fair to share my opinion on the matter.

I compose, yes, it is true. I invent fictions that order time and relate experience. But for what reason do I invite others into this task?

I only seek to illuminate a goodness that I fear—

[The rest is too heavily scratched out to translate. Sorry, Ed. I hope that suffices. Onto the next . . .]

May 30, 1892

Allegro. Tomorrow night will tell all.

Fast, too fast, time is hurtling towards its end. And what can I do? Burn. That is all.

I must burn that which I invented.

The thing will not change, cannot change the Tsar's mind. But perhaps the action, so futile, will suggest other possibilities.

And yet, I am wracked with guilt. If I kill the thing, can the spirit endure? No. I know the answer even before I act.

But burn it must.

I visited Sofia's grave today. It was no heavy burden. I laid chamomile upon her brow. I can only hope that it brings her rest.

Standing, I saw the strangest thing. A man, small in stature, leaping over gravestones.

I do not burn with a heavy soul, I thought.

Perhaps there is still possibility in this sculpture.

There was a time when I believed in self-evidence. But no longer. I burn with lightness.

In My Grandfather's Day

It is nearly impossible to summarize a book and, likewise, to analyze one of Eco's works is a voluminous task. In an effort to limit the scope of what I can accomplish, I propose to perform a close reading of one chapter. This chapter is, I think, the most important for the way in which it shamelessly constructs Simonini's psyche.[40] First his mother as "woman," then his grandfather as anti-Semitic, and finally his father as anti-Jesuit and conspiracy theorist all shape the protagonist in ways that reverberate throughout *The Prague Cemetery*. It is as if one is reading the opening lines of Marcus Aurelius' *Meditations*: "From my grandfather Verus: goodness of character and freedom from anger."[41] But rather than curating virtue, Simonini is collecting visions of hate, racism, and bigotry. And while Simonini is performing psychoanalysis upon himself, I am doing no such thing.[42] I am, rather, reading the chapter, "In My Grandfather's Day,"[43] through the theorizing lens that I set out in Part I of *Narrativizing Theories*. The reason for choosing this chapter over others is simple: in it, I find a confluence of those *as-if-it-is* narratives that Simonini commits to (implicit religion), which are central to my understanding of an aesthetics of ambiguity. "In My Grandfather's Day," in the end, is a test case for what has come before. And if it seems strange to you that my playground is of a literary nature, then I will leave this introduction with a small

---

40. Spruyt, "Umberto Eco's *The Prague Cemetery*," 4.

41. Gill, trans., *Marcus Aurelius: Meditations*, 3.

42. For a good psychoanalytic reading, see Spruyt, "Umberto Eco's *The Prague Cemetery*."

43. Eco, "In My Grandfather's Day," 47–82.

reminder: both Winkler, and Eco before her, find literature to be *the place* for examining the functions of ambiguity.[44]

From My Mother: Woman as Cultural Unit

How does one construct or encounter an encyclopedia, twist it into a narrative, and then embody it?[45] If the reader moves too quickly, then she will miss it. "My childhood," the chapter begins. "Turin . . . A hillside on the other bank of the Po, me on a balcony with my mother. Then she was gone, and my father was crying . . . My grandfather said it was God's will."[46] This is all that the text says of Simonini's mother, who is nothing more than a specter to the protagonist, a figure of loss. And yet her absence reverberates throughout Simonini's earliest memories. "Childhood," he writes:

> for me was my grandfather, more than my father and mother. I hated my mother who had gone without telling me, I hated my father who had done nothing to stop her, I hated God because he had willed such a thing to happen, and I hated my grandfather because he thought it normal for God to will such things.[47]

And so, it appears, that Simonini's *cogito* has its roots in the disappearance of his mother.

Simonini is left, young and blank except for the hate that roils within him. His encyclopedia is constructed, cut off from the world,[48] as if he were an empty vessel awaiting the cultural units and interpretants of his grandfather and father. While the experiences with and moral lectures from his remaining family members certainly created the cultural units of <<Mother>>[49] and <<Woman>> in Simonini's encyclopedia, they are not the only encounters that contributed to the complex web of Simonini's commitments.

---

44. Winkler, *Ambiguity: Language and Communication*, 18; and Eco, *A Theory*, 261.

45. This can, of course, work the other way around. One can have an encounter with the material world and from that construct an encyclopedia.

46. Eco, *The Prague Cemetery*, 47.

47. Eco, *The Prague Cemetery*, 47.

48. Eco, *The Prague Cemetery*, 64: "When I reached eighteen, my grandfather, who wanted me to be a lawyer . . . resigned himself to letting me out of the house and sending me to university. This was my first chance to mix with boys my own age, but it was too late, and I felt uneasy around them."

49. As a reminder, the <<X>> construction refers to the content of a given cultural unit and neither the spoken word nor thing in itself.

Since he did not attend public school, Simonini was educated by Jesuits brought into his home at the behest of his grandfather. One such priest, Father Bergamaschi, taught him the evils of communism. Babette of Interlaken, he told Simonini, was known as the "Great Virgin of Swiss Communism."[50] She was beyond salvation as a debauched and thieving murderer. "Babette, her blond hair blowing in the wind," the priest said, "like the Whore of Babylon, concealed beneath her mantle of charms the fact that she was the herald of secret societies, the demon who orchestrated all the tricks and intrigues of those mysterious confraternities."[51] With enchantment and thaumaturgy, Babette could overwhelm men and governments alike. It was assumed, given her knack for controlling the powerful, that she was possessed by Satan.

And how does Simonini respond? What does he store away inside his encyclopedia? He was shocked and horrified but could not stop himself from dreaming of Babette. "I wanted to block out the pictures of that blond demon . . . surely naked, that demonic, fragrant hobgoblin, her breasts heaving rapturously with godless, sinful pride."[52] Yet, Simonini admits, he wants to model her, imitate her, and be like her. He, too, desires to be "a secret and all-powerful agent who forged passports and led victims of the other sex to perdition."[53] That which terrifies Simonini, he yearns to become so that he can destroy it as it exists as an *other*. Simonini's cultural unit <<Woman>> is filled with absence, lust, and debauchery but also an enticing mystery. <<Woman>> is something other to be hated and feared, consigned to nightmares of passion.

The final encounter in Simonini's youth that contributed to the construction of his cultural unit <<Woman>> was when he was shown, by a companion, a nineteenth-century *Playboy*. "I shuddered as I turned the pages and found engravings," Simonini writes, "that sent streams of sweat trickling from my hair down to my cheeks and neck."[54] He cannot recall how that "turbulent" night ended, but he does pull from the recesses of his mind an old scrap of wisdom stored in the encyclopedia of his childhood. "All this feminine charm," he chants to himself, "is nothing but phlegm, blood, humors, bile . . . how can we ever want to embrace a sack of excrement?"[55]

50. Eco, *The Prague Cemetery*, 63.
51. Eco, *The Prague Cemetery*, 63.
52. Eco, *The Prague Cemetery*, 63.
53. Eco, *The Prague Cemetery*, 63.
54. Eco, *The Prague Cemetery*, 74.
55. Eco, *The Prague Cemetery*, 75.

Added to Simonini's <<Woman>> is her physiology. <<Woman>> is nothing more nor less than fluid and waste. It is shocking, no doubt, for many readers of the twenty-first century to encounter Simonini's words. As shocking for him to conceive of <<Woman>> in other terms. If I approach Simonini through ambiguity, however—rather than only revulsion and fear—then I can see ambiguity working on two levels. Ambiguity is an awareness that the encyclopedia, which allows for understanding and the embodied world given as reality, is cognized into a narrative that is and can only be *as if*.

The first level of ambiguity for Simonini is the ambiguity that he encounters as a protagonist. His mother gone; he is raised in a world of men. Discovering women throughout his adolescence can only result in ambiguous entanglements—moments when the material world added, stretched, or altered his encyclopedic entry on <<Woman>>. The second level of Simonini's ambiguity is that of the reader's, in so far as Simonini represents ambiguity itself. To a reader who adheres to modern, Western-liberal values, Simonini likely repulses. She does not want Simonini to construct his encyclopedia—or have it constructed—in such a way that <<Woman>> is disparaged. For this reader, ambiguity is the terrifying prospect of accepting Simonini's encyclopedia into the Universal Encyclopedia of human construction. Simonini is ambiguous because he confronts the reader's assumptions and challenges her. Not to hate women, but to reconcile herself to the possibility that hate is a human—as opposed to monstrous—reality. The abhorrence of Simonini is a line of resistance that the reader cannot escape.

This realization or encounter with the event of ambiguity leads to a state of ambiguity wherein a reader can foresee the many paths of cultural units and their interpretants, in all their potentiality, collapse into one, singular, committed narrative—or implicit religion. Even if distasteful or destructive, a chosen and embodied cultural arrangement is a possible or valid instantiation of the cultural encyclopedia as it exists in total.

Encyclopedias lead to narratives that are embodied in the world by the way in which the reader arranges her experiences through cultural units. These narratives proliferate, through their interpretants, into infinity and coexist as equiprobable—but they always return to the Dynamical Object, telling the reader something more of her world. As repugnant as it is, Simonini's narrative is as valid[56]—in so far as it is a narratival construction—as the readers. The cogency of his narrative is neutral, so long as the reader grants Simonini his starting points. And how can she not? The confrontation

---

56. I discuss "validity" more fully below.

of one arrangement or set of commitments with another is a coexistent incompatibility that exists on the plane of expression or semiosphere and is embodied in the world. But the semiosphere knows nothing of right or wrong. It knows only choice—the decisions made, the committed narratives, that embody in the world. It explains, but it cannot judge, for judgment only happens granted the starting point of another, equiprobable, narrative of commitment.

The arrangement of Simonini's encyclopedia could always be different, however. The way in which Simonini sorts, organizes, and makes palatable his committed narrative is a choice. He is not bound by the already present and ever-existing encyclopedias of his grandfather and father, even though they pull as strongly as the Tiber. Any encounter with ambiguity affords Simonini the opportunity to choose otherwise.

This choice, revealed in the state of ambiguity, leads to the consideration of <<Accountability>> and <<Responsibility>>. But these are difficult encyclopedic entries laden with their own cultural interpretants. And yet, I can conceive of no other way to articulate choice. When in the non-judgmental space of ambiguity that has been instigated by an ambiguous encounter, I am presented with equiprobable choices. From one node to another, the path that I traverse is an alternative that I am both accountable to and responsible for. Even given the circumstances of his youth, Simonini is answerable for <<Woman>> and the way in which he embodies or commits to his arranged narrative. The interplay between an already given encyclopedia, a lived experience, and a constructed, as-if narrative, which all point to the provisionality of knowledge and the narrativization of reality, do not, by necessity, result in the abdication of ethics. There are lines of resistance written into every hermeneutical cluster.[57] While all narratival arrangements are equiprobable in the non-judgmental space of ambiguity, not all are equally convincing once chosen and submitted to the community for ratification.[58]

From My Grandfather: Mordechai the Monster

Simonini learned, from his grandfather, how Abbé Barruel planted seeds of universal conspiracy. For this abbot, the Knight Templars and Freemasons were at fault—of nearly everything in the world. But it was clear to Simonini's grandfather, Giovanni Battista Simonini,[59] that the abbot had mis-

57. Peters, *Sigurd's Lament*, 52–58.
58. I say more about this below.
59. From here on out, I will refer to Simonini's grandfather, Giovanni Battista

represented the scope of the universal conspiracy. Barruel had forgotten the Jews and their desire to "destroy the name of Christ wherever possible."[60] It was the Jews, Giovanni argued, that stood behind all plots, pulling the strings of power.

But how could Giovanni know this? He had heard it from the Jews themselves.[61] What follows is disturbing but, as Eco writes, "the only fictitious character in this story is the protagonist, Simone Simonini. His grandfather . . . is not invented."[62] The characters in *The Prague Cemetery*, in fact, "actually existed, and said and did what they are described as saying and doing in this novel."[63] The <<Jew>> then, as an entry into Simonini's encyclopedia, was mercilessly and meticulously constructed by Giovanni's own creation, the exiled Jew, Mordechai.

"If you don't behave yourself and go straight to sleep," Giovanni would threaten Simonini, "the horrible Mordechai will come visit you tonight."[64] Young and scared, Simonini would imagine Mordechai, "dribbling lubriciously, muttering, 'Fee-fi-fo-fum, I smell the blood of a Christian boy.'"[65] And what was this story that so terrified a little boy from Turin and contributed to his cultural unit <<Jew>>?

Let me suggest, first, that the text here, reprehensible no doubt, is asking something of its reader. It is asking her to enter into the mind of Simonini, who is hate, racism, and violence. He is everything that the reader hopes she is not. But the text asks the reader to enter into the mind of Simonini, for a time, and participate in the construction of intolerance.

Is this task acceptable? Even for a novel? For a genre that reveres decorum? If the task of an aesthetics of ambiguity is to examine the narrative paths that humans traverse, then when should it turn back in the fear of legitimizing that which it only seeks to understand?

When does ambiguity overstep?

Mordechai was a Syrian Jew suspected of murdering an Arab boy. Found in a ditch, the body was "cut into a thousand pieces and pounded in a mortar."[66] It was likely, Giovanni thought, that Mordechai had falsely baptized the child for use in Passover, because Jews needed Christian blood

---

Simonini, as Giovanni.

60. Eco, *The Prague Cemetery*, 52.
61. Eco, *The Prague Cemetery*, 52.
62. Eco, *The Prague Cemetery*, 438.
63. Eco, *The Prague Cemetery*, 438.
64. Eco, *The Prague Cemetery*, 58.
65. Eco, *The Prague Cemetery*, 58.
66. Eco, *The Prague Cemetery*, 54.

to make their bread. But Mordechai could not find a Christian boy, so he settled for a baptized Arab. Baptism, you see, is efficacious regardless who performs it. So unwittingly, and even though Satan himself assuredly stood behind it, the Arab boy was saved and committed into heaven.

Tortured by the police, Mordechai finally confessed. Five other Jews were rounded up and executed, but Mordechai was set free with "dislocated limbs."[67] After a series of unfortunate events, he arrived in Turin and met Giovanni. It was there that Simonini's grandfather first learned of the Jews' universal plot. For Mordechai:

> told him how their Talmud preached hatred of the Christian race, and how in order to corrupt the Christians, they, the Jews, had invented Freemasonry, of which he had become one of their nameless superiors, and that he commanded lodges from Naples to London, but he had to remain hidden, living in secret, segregated from the world, so as not to get knifed by the Jesuits, who were hunting for him everywhere . . . [but the Jews had] vowed to become rulers of the world in less than a century, to abolish all other sects so that theirs would reign supreme, to build as many synagogues as there were Christian churches and to reduce everyone else to slavery.[68]

Giovanni, utilizing synecdoche, ended in a flourish: "I had learned from all of them what, in fact, I had heard from one man alone."[69]

Poured into Simonini's cultural unit <<Jew>> was, first, that there was a universal plot to overtake and rule the systems of the world. This plot was instigated by the Jews and had been in motion for centuries. The Jew would stop at nothing to achieve her goal. Added to this was the depiction of the Jew as a drinker of blood, someone who was both merciless and immoral. And, given Mordechai's absolute dedication to his plot, Giovanni characterized the Jew as inhuman. Yes, Giovanni wrote the entry for <<Jew>>, which was then stored away in Simonini's cultural encyclopedia. But he also achieved something else. He constructed an enemy for Simonini.

A young man's encyclopedia is written for him—not out of nothing, but through the texts of his community—in such a way that he then acts out or embodies various cultural units in the created reality that he has experienced and chosen. To him, this construction is absolute. For the encyclopedia as the cultural repertoire of a given society, as its historical memory, "is based on the conviction that there can be no meaning, or

---

67. Eco, *The Prague Cemetery*, 54.
68. Eco, *The Prague Cemetery*, 55–56.
69. Eco, *The Prague Cemetery*, 56.

language or culture outside and independently of the community in which the speakers are defined and exist."[70] To Simonini then, the <<Jew>> is and can only be the enemy.

This is not only a construction of <<Jew>>, but also a glimpse into the construction of Simonini's identity. "Having an enemy," Eco writes, "is important not only to define our identity but also to provide us with an obstacle against which to measure our system of values and, in seeking to overcome it, to demonstrate our own worth. So when there is no enemy, we have to invent one."[71] Any notion that the Jews, in any way, resemble the characters in *The Protocols of the Elders of Zion* is patently false. It is pure invention. And yet, for Giovanni, and subsequently Simonini, it is wholly true. The <<Jew>> as a cultural unit is diabolical. This "fact" not only contributes to Simonini's store of cultural knowledge but also allows him to measure his system of values. In seeing <<Jew>> through his grandfather's cultural unit, Simonini is able to establish a counterweight to his own identity. He can overcome the <<Jew>>, his enemy, and "demonstrate his own worth."[72] This is clear, as an example, when Simonini describes his first meetings with Froïde.

"He sat alone at a nearby table," Simonini writes:

> and at first we limited ourselves to polite nods. I judged him to be gloomy by nature, ill at ease, timidly eager for someone to confide in, to unburden his anxieties . . . but I had always remained aloof . . . I nevertheless knew that all Jews who live and make money in Paris have German names, and, my suspicions having been raised by his hooked nose . . . 'I prefer to keep my distance—Jew and German are a mix I don't much like.'[73]

And again:

> There are Paris intellectuals who, before expressing their distaste for Jews, concede that some of their best friends are Jews. Hypocrisy. I have no Jewish friends (God forbid). All my life I've avoided Jews. Perhaps I have instinctively avoided them, because the Jew (like the German) can be identified by his smell . . . This and other signs help them to recognize each other, as pederasts do. My grandfather used to say that their smell is due to the excessive use of garlic and onion . . . But it must also be

---

70. Santambrogio and Violi, "Introduction," 22.
71. Eco, *Inventing the Enemy*, 2.
72. Eco, *Inventing the Enemy*, 2.
73. Eco, *Inventing the Enemy*, 37.

the race itself—their infected blood, their feeble loins. They are all communists.[74]

Yet the reader knows, or will know by the next chapter, that Simonini's dislike of Jews has nothing to do with instinct, unless she is willing to say that one's encyclopedia has an instinctual effect upon the embodying individual. The point, however, is that regardless of what Simonini may think of Froïde, he believes the opposite of himself. "He has a hooked nose," Simonini might say, "but not like me. I have no such contorted appendage." The Jew, or <<Jew>>, is nothing more than a cultural unit by which Simonini can construct his own, superior identity.

The <<Jew>> is constructed out of the bibliography of Giovanni for a young Simonini, who will, no doubt, add his own texts to the entry.[75] Can Simonini be forgiven for this? And, if so, who will absolve him? Or is Simonini accountable to and responsible for the cultural units that comprise his reality? To ask it differently, when does the non-judgmental space of ambiguity cross into the judgmental reality of communal life? How does one judge between competing narratives, especially when those narratives are already given?

From My Father: The Jesuit as Pedophile

Simonini's father is absent. He is often gone, fighting with the Carbonari, Italian nationalists seeking an independent, constitutionally ruled republic. Perhaps this is because of his lost wife or because his father, Giovanni, was an ardent monarchist and, by all accounts, an oppressive and demanding personality who supported the Jesuits then under attack by republican gangs. Giovanni, in fact, sees the emerging Italian republic as "the advent of the Antichrist," an event instigated by Jewish intrigue and the plots of Mordechai.[76] Whatever the reason, when Simonini's father is present, he is often distracted and lethargic.

Simonini's encyclopedia is shaped in two significant ways by his father. The first is when Simonini discovers his father's cache of popular culture concealed in Giovanni's attic.[77] Inside are the formative novels, newspapers, and *feuilletons* of Simonini's youth. Chief among them is his father's *Le Constitutionnel*, which serialized Eugène Sue's *The Wandering Jew*. "It was

---

74. Eco, *Inventing the Enemy*, 38.
75. Eco, *Inventing the Enemy*, 57: "I pass the flame of witness on to you."
76. Eco, *Inventing the Enemy*, 67.
77. Eco, *Inventing the Enemy*, 75.

here," Simonini writes, "that I learned how the infamous Society of Jesus had managed to plot the most abominable crimes to seize an inheritance, trampling on the rights of poor, good people."[78]

After Simonini learns of the Jesuit's "plot" in the attic of his grandfather—Eco's protagonists are always stumbling upon important cultural artifacts in the attics of his novels—his encyclopedic entries on <<Jesuits>> and <<Priests>> are solidified by those rare moments of interaction between him and his father. "I hated the [Jesuit] teacher of the moment, not just because his way of teaching was by rapping my knuckles, but also because my father . . . had instilled in me a hatred of priests."[79] And what was this hatred comprised of?

> It is Jesuitism that undermines, torments, afflicts, vilifies, persecutes, destroys men of free spirit; it is Jesuitism that drives good and valiant men out of public positions and replaces them with others who are base and contemptible; it is Jesuitism that slackens, obstructs, torments, harasses, confuses, weakens, corrupts public and private education in a thousand ways . . . [after an incredibly long list of that which Jesuitism is responsible][80] . . . No sect in the world is so gutless . . . so hard and ruthless when its own interests are at stake, as the Company of Jesus . . . the Jesuits of Italy kill the soul with their tongues, like reptiles, or with their pens.[81]

And here, two thoughts strike Simonini: One, pens have the power to shape reality. And two, encyclopedias are fluid. "I have always been amused," Simonini's father tells him, "Gioberti took some of these ideas secondhand from *The Wandering Jew*."[82] Gioberti is the writer of a text wherein Simonini's father first encountered the "true nature" of the Jesuits, ideas repurposed from a novel.

Simonini learns from his father what will become a lifelong practice, to take what is already known in a culture's encyclopedia and twist it ever so slightly in order to manipulate and contort a given cultural unit. Between the pen and the recycling of cultural knowledge, Simonini is able to construct the lies of *The Protocols of the Elders of Zion*. He later admits as much:

78. Eco, *Inventing the Enemy*, 66.
79. Eco, *Inventing the Enemy*, 59.
80. Cf. Eco, *The Infinity of Lists*, on the function of lists in literature.
81. Eco, *The Prague Cemetery*, 61.
82. Eco, *The Prague Cemetery*, 61.

if I wanted to sell the story of conspiracy, I didn't have to offer the buyer anything original, but simply something he already knew or could have found out more easily in other ways. People believe only what they already know, and this is the beauty of the Universal Form of Conspiracy.[83]

And, I might add, the importance of understanding ambiguity, which expands the already known.

The <<Jesuits>> then are violent liars and manipulators "dressed up as women." They are hypocrites who use their positions of religious authority to wield and exploit power to their own ends. They are even, Simonini suggests, pedophiles who seek out tutoring positions so that they can touch little boys.[84] They are all this and more, for they too are entangled in the universal plot to conquer the world.

To what do all of these cultural units in Simonini's encyclopedia add? "I have known many people who feared the conspiracy of some hidden enemy," he writes:

> for my grandfather it was the Jews, for the Jesuits it was the Masons, for my Garibaldian father it was the Jesuits... Who knows how many other people in this world still think they are being threatened by some conspiracy? Here's a form to be filled out at will, by each person with his own conspiracy... No one believes their misfortunes are attributable to any shortcomings of their own; that is why they must find a culprit. Dumas offers, to the frustration of everyone (individuals as well as countries), the explanation for their failure. It was someone else, on Thunder Mountain, who planned your ruin.[85]

The cultural units of Simonini are tools by which he can turn the encyclopedia to his own ends, manipulate the populace, and wield his own form of power. <<Women>> are seductresses. <<Jews>> are sinister. <<Jesuits>> are hypocritical pedophiles. Simonini, however, is outside of it all, pulling the strings of history. But what he fails to realize is that his encyclopedia, too, was constructed, organized, and maneuvered in such a way that his narrative was already written. And it is this failure—of self-reflection?—that leads Simonini to overlook his encounter with ambiguity and his confrontation with choice.

83. Eco, *The Prague Cemetery*, 79.
84. Eco, *The Prague Cemetery*, 64.
85. Eco, *The Prague Cemetery*, 78.

Ambiguity and Thing

At nearly fourteen,[86] Simonini has his first encounter with an ambiguity that violates, challenges, and invents. It is accountable to *a reality*, but not irreducibly so, as it also has the potential for opening significations of the material world. Ambiguity is strategically produced and employed through creative contradictions in the already given cultural encyclopedia, contradictions that not only transform and expand the code, but also change the material world—not just my perceptions of it. Ambiguity is that which reveals, highlights, or brings my attention to the provisionality or the as-if-ness of the narrative that I take for granted. It is also that space in which I can analyze my own provisional assumptions and begin to account for the potentiality of other ways of seeing and doing.

Simonini's code is comprised of the cultural units written for him by his grandfather and father—<<Woman>>, <<Jew>>, <<Jesuit>>—and then stitched together to form a narrative of embodiment. It is the task of an aesthetics of ambiguity informed by materiality and implicit religion to show or reveal the various narratival constructions to which humans commit, the way in which any set of cultural units are arranged into a string that constitutes a narrative that can be embodied in the world of things. Sometimes these narratives correspond to the empirical world, often, however, they contradict it. This is not to say that the material world is the only world or the "correct" reality, but that it produces lines of resistance that, if I allow them, keep me within the boundary of perceptual interpretation rather than overdetermination foisted upon the world from an already given, though invented, cultural encyclopedia.

I might think, given *Dumbo*, that elephants use their floppy ears to fly. But when provided with the line of resistance that is the material world, I must either check myself into Bedlam or rearrange my cultural encyclopedia—even as I must also admit *Dumbo* as an interpretant into my construction of the cultural unit <<Elephant>>. When this confrontation with a line of resistance happens, when an already given encyclopedia is confronted with that which is ambiguous, then my already arranged, as-if narrative has the potential to be unmasked as provisional. It is in that moment, in that space of ambiguity, that the possibility for choosing differently arises. I can traverse alternative paths. I can construct my encyclopedia otherwise. I can, through abduction, negotiate a new narrative that will, until I stumble upon another line of resistance, remain provisional.

Simonini's encyclopedic narrative as arranged by his grandfather and father represent *a reality*. And though distasteful to many modern, Western

---

86. Eco, *The Prague Cemetery*, 58.

readers, it is a reality that cannot be dismissed as either atypical or unworthy of consideration. It is, in other alarming words, one valid reality among many. By valid, however, I do not mean either "correct" or "true," but rather consistent with an arranged set of cultural units. Valid, here, is not a value judgment. Imagine the key of "C" in music. If, given "C," I want to play the twelve bar blues, then I must, according to tradition, play the corresponding IV and V chords, "F" and "G." In the key of "C" then, "F" and "G" are absolute and valid for that which I set out to accomplish. I cannot play "A" or "B" and hope to arrive back at "C" without dissonance and confusion. Changing the key, however, allows me to maintain the arrangement of the twelve-bar blues while utilizing a different set of absolute and valid chords. In "C" though, I am bound by the IV and the V. To make that claim is not to make a value judgment. The key of "C" is what it is, even if music—through ambiguity?—affords a key change via a common chord.

Simonini's encyclopedic narrative is valid in the sense that the key of "C" is a valid key in which to play the twelve bar blues.[87] That which comprises the key of "C" is absolute, but not for all of the potential occurrences of a given twelve bar blues arrangement. I can play "Kind Hearted Woman," in either "C" or "G" depending on my mood, context, or desire. So, yes, Simonini's code is valid, if reprehensible, which leads me to the question: How do I judge between competing narratives? How do I decide to play in either "C" or "G?"

Simonini, approaching fourteen, wanders the limits of Piedmont's ghetto. It is there that he meets:

> a girl with black hair who crosses piazza Carlina each morning carrying a basket covered with a cloth to a nearby shop. Fiery gaze, velvet eyes, dark complexion . . . Impossible that she's a Jewess, that those men my grandfather has described, with rapacious features and venomous eyes, could produce a woman like her. And yet she can only have come from the ghetto.[88]

This is the first time, Simonini admits, that he has looked upon a woman. His heart pounds. His palms sweat. He becomes enraptured by her sight. She is, for Simonini, the embodiment of ambiguity, cutting across his arranged, as-if narrative. His encounter in the material world, gives a line of resistance, provides him a glimpse into an alternate reality. And for a moment, Simonini—*Odi ergo sum*—appears human. What can he do? Can he rearrange his

---

87. I do not think that one can defer to a concept of beauty here—that one rendition of the twelve-bar blues is more beautiful than another. For what is beauty but a subject category that I wield to prop up my own encyclopedia?

88. Eco, *The Prague Cemetery*, 59.

encyclopedia? Can he reject the wisdom of his grandfather? Can he traverse an alternate path and embody a different as-if narrative?

In that liminal space of ambiguity, Simonini realizes the equiprobability of his encyclopedia. He is afforded the possibility of playing in a different key. And what does he do? "One morning I dare to stop the girl and, eyes lowered, ask her if I can help carry her basket."[89] He challenges his narrative! He seeks out a change in key. But, according to Simonini:

> she replies haughtily, in dialect, that she can manage perfectly well by herself. But she doesn't call me *manssü*, but *gagnu*, boy . . . I've been humiliated by a daughter of Zion. Is it perhaps because I'm fat? This, in fact, marks the beginning of my war against the daughters of Eve.[90]

Simonini rejects ambiguity. He falls back into his key and commits—then and there—to embody the arranged, as-if narrative that he has received. In that moment, however fleeting though, he had a choice between the unforeseen potentiality of untraversed paths and the already known and given encyclopedia. What would have come of *The Protocols of the Elders of Zion* had Simonini chosen differently? If he had swallowed his pride and seen the "fiery gaze" of the other as a welcomed violation of his culture's code? But Simonini committed himself to the already written, and the horrific tale of violence, hate, and racism continued.

An aesthetics of ambiguity allows me to peel back the layers of an embodied, as-if narrative and its various encounters with the world of things. It is also an exercise in understanding. This understanding is not a stamp of approval. It is a negotiation in the ambiguous, cultural world of encyclopedias. Simonini's choice is abhorrent, but a choice nevertheless. And it is this choice, and my willingness to condemn it, that betray the judgmental side of ambiguity. I choose, because I must. But how is it that I can choose *one* narrative? What allows me to call one encyclopedic arrangement abhorrent over against another, equiprobable arrangement? My arranged, as-if narrative and the community of interpreters in which I find myself. There is no standard of judgment that stands outside of all encyclopedias.

We are all responsible and accountable.

And in so far as Simonini seeks to integrate his encyclopedia into the global repository of knowledge, I can—much like merging a pull request from GitHub[91]—reject it. This is similar to the European Union saying to Turkey, "If you want to join the EU, then you must do *x*, *y*, and *z*. You must adopt and then embody our encyclopedia." The choice is Turkey's alone,

---

89. Eco, *The Prague Cemetery*, 59.
90. Eco, *The Prague Cemetery*, 59.
91. "Merging a Pull Request from GitHub."

but one for which—in terms of the outcome—they are responsible for and accountable to.

Simonini's narrative is despicable to me, and many others, because I refuse to embody it. But as Will Eisner has shown in *The Plot: The Secret Story of The Protocols of the Elders of Zion*, many others have not. And, while that is more than just disheartening, what can I (or Eisner or Eco) do other than strategically create confrontations with ambiguity?

Conclusion

Ambiguity reveals, highlights, and brings my attention to the provisionality or the as-if-ness of the narratives that I take for granted. It is also a space in which I can analyze my own provisional assumptions and begin to account for the potentiality of other ways of seeing and doing. The task of an aesthetics of ambiguity is to examine an already given cultural encyclopedia—a narrativizing theory—to reveal, analyze, and understand the as-if narratives that humans embody.

Simonini's repugnance forces a certain kind of reader to ask, self-reflexively, how she, herself chooses or judges between competing, though equiprobable narratives? Since ambiguity instigates the possibility for constructing and embodying different narrativized theories, the choice of which narrative to traverse ultimately lies with the individual navigating ambiguous spaces. She is not alone, however, for when she enters back into the communal world, she must seek to ratify her choices with an already present interpretive community. The larger the community (like the European Union), the more power it has to force an already given, co-constructed, as-if reality.

The choices I make as an individual or as a member of a ratifying community are choices that I am both accountable to and responsible for. There is no one, no community, or no *thing* that stands outside of cultural units, encyclopedias, and as-if narratives to which a Universal Encyclopedia can defer.

We are our own legislators and judges. That which we choose and then embody is on our heads alone. To seek something outside of the encyclopedia is to abdicate both choice and responsibility.[92] It is to construct a narrativizing theory that abolishes lines of resistance. It is to embody a reality in which elephants fly. It is to forgo the open, plurivocality of ambiguity for the totalizing, univocality of dogma. It is a refusal to maintain provisionality.

---

92. The question still might be raised, to what are we responsible? To which I can only answer—to choice and the narrative.

Excursus Two
The Kingdom

> I'm an agnostic writer who wants to know what exactly Christians believe today. If you want to share that with me, I'd be delighted; if not, I won't bother you any longer.
>
> —Emmanuel Carrère, *The Kingdom*

Introduction

> Between the word of God and my understanding, it's the word of God that counts, and it would be silly of me to retain only what jibes with my limited understanding. Never forget: it's the Gospel that judges me, not the opposite.[1]

CREATIVE NONFICTION IS A burgeoning field. It is not the place of this excursus to convince you of that. It is the place, however, to argue that creative nonfiction and ambiguity go hand-in-hand. To write true stories with literary and artistic style in such a way that the events are verifiable, even if the writer is entangled with the narrative, is to write with an intrinsic understanding of ambiguity. That which happened is ordered and arranged in such a way that the telling cannot be separated from the event. To critique a thing as "not true" or to say that "it didn't happen that way" is to misunderstand this ambiguous genre.

It is my argument that creative nonfiction is a genre of ambiguity, and that this is reflected in Emmanuel Carrère's work, *The Kingdom*. If there is an underlying assumption to this excursus, then it is that academic interdisciplinarity can learn much from Carrère and should adopt his style as a means for expressing its liminal insights.

---

1. Carrère, *The Kingdom*, 33–34.

A Disappointing Faith

> I'm tempted to be ironic about the person I was, but I want to remember the confusion and terror I felt at the thought that the faith that had changed my life and to which I held above all else was endangered.[2]

While there are many creative nonfiction stories to choose from, Emmanuel Carrère's *The Kingdom* is a fitting companion for a book on an aesthetics of ambiguity that is also concerned with implicit religion. A novel in four parts, *The Kingdom* recounts the story of Emmanuel Carrère's own brush with faith and subsequent spiral into doubt before historiographically tackling Paul, Luke, and the writing of the Gospels. Though perhaps discomfiting to some, *The Kingdom* is a work of creative nonfiction that, among many other things, problematizes the porous borders between fiction and history.

While one can recognize the intense research and analysis that went into writing it, one cannot help but read *The Kingdom*, and subsequently the *Gospel of Luke*, through the thoughtful eyes of Carrère. *The Kingdom* is a work of both history and *poesis* that seeks to display the first-century Mediterranean world in all of its complexity while also projecting Carrère's emotion and context onto the record that it is trying to elucidate. And it is the essence of Carrère's projection that captures ambiguity. For in Carrère's deft hands, faith is not only defamiliarized, but so too the Gospels, their meaning, and the very idea of Christ.

Attending Easter Sunday at an Abbey during his intensely Christian period, Carrère writes:

> The chapel is gray and ugly, lit by a dull light. The thick stone walls drip with humidity. The community now has no more than ten or so nuns, all old and wobbly on their feet . . . their voices falter and crack as they sing, and the bleating of the young priest who looks like the village idiot and who's come to bring them Communion isn't any better . . . no one really seems to be listening . . . Mass with the nuns isn't exactly cheerful. In fact, it's enough to fill you with sadness, and it would have sent me packing in the past—supposing I'd ever gone in there in the first place . . . But I say to myself: This is it, this is the kingdom. Everything that is weak, despised, and wanting: that is the dwelling place of Christ . . . But what if I were chased out? Or, worse still,

---

2. Carrère, *The Kingdom*, 69.

if I were happy to leave? If one day I considered this time . . . an embarrassing episode.³

It is the tension between time and memory that makes this pericope so ambiguous. I know that Carrère is agnostic and that he is honestly trying to recall this time in his life without irony. I can see both his commitment and his disappointment, his hope and his sadness. There is a desire to hold fast to faith, while also an admission that—even then—he will not. And while Carrère is ambiguous in that he is problematizing, challenging, and violating all kinds of codes, he is also self-reflexive, and light. There is a weightiness to his writing that is neither heavy nor dense. The priest is a jester. The nuns are stoics. And the place of infinite hope is dark and dank. I cannot help but read this—seriously, soberly—but with the hint of a smile. I can visualize the chapel, its inhabitants, and I can see, too, Carrère, desperately frustrated by his own lack of desire and self-conscience to the point of embarrassment.

I cannot forget this scene of disappointed and waning faith as I move into Carrère's historically researched and retold *Gospel of Luke*. It is the scenes of sad and depressing Christianity two-thousand years later that, in fact, shape my reading of Carrère's gospel. It is the intentional structuring of the work that is itself ambiguous, in that it continually questions, probes, and violates its own encyclopedia. It is ambiguous in that it ends with a question, which forces the reader to do the hard work of constructing meaning even if, as Carrère suggests in his epilogue, he has missed the point or is "completely off the mark."⁴

The Gospel according to Luke Carrère

Maybe that's how it happened. Or . . . I think I have a better idea.⁵

Deep into his narrativizing of Luke's journalistic account of the life of Paul, Carrère discusses the two-year stay of the latter in Caesarea. It is here that Carrère begins to weave a tale of Luke's sleuth-like piecing together of Jesus's life. Carrère knows he is creating, admits it but—as a writer of creative nonfiction—claims there is little else that he could do. "Everything I've told until now," Carrère writes, "is known and more or less accepted."⁶ True. He writes both eloquently and well about the beginnings of the Christ movement. He does not mislead. But then? "For [those] two years . . . I've got nothing. Not

---

3. Carrère, *The Kingdom*, 70–72.
4. Carrère, *The Kingdom*, 378.
5. Carrère, *The Kingdom*, 98.
6. Carrère, *The Kingdom*, 196.

a single source. I'm free—and forced—to invent."[7] Carrère's project then becomes "to investigate what [Luke's] investigation *may* have been like."[8]

Is this history or a fresh ordering of data by a creative imagination? It's a little of both. History is always an ordering after the fact. It's that which I believe to be true about a given event, which could change in accordance with new information. History is fluid. And it's history's fluidity that allows Carrère to invent where necessary. He has compiled the data, but it is yet to be ordered.

How shall it be arranged? Why, by Carrère's own encyclopedia, of course. And is that any different from what I have done? No. For I, too, collected, arranged, and organized through a particular encyclopedia, narrativizing theory, and embodied experience. I, too, have my moments where I am forced to invent.

And yet, invention is not a free for all. It is an accounting of that which presents itself to me. It is playing at Firstness through Thirdness, which is all I have anyway. It is an admission that narrativizing theories are revealed as provisional only when they have encountered the openness and potentiality of ambiguity.

"No," Carrère writes, "I don't believe that Jesus was resurrected. I don't believe that a man came back from the dead."[9] Even though he had earlier admitted that the resurrection was the only truth upon which a life should be founded. "But the fact that people do believe it," he continues:

> and that I believed it myself—intrigues, fascinates, troubles, and moves me—I don't know which verb is the most appropriate. I'm writing this book to avoid thinking that now that I no longer believe, I know better than those who do, and better than my former self when I believed. I'm writing this book to avoid coming down too firmly in my favor.[10]

Carrère once believed. He no longer does. And those that still do? They are ambiguous to Carrère. While he uses a string of different verbs, he could have said that they violate, challenge, and question his encyclopedia. That, through them, he is forced to consider their differences, commitments, and narrativizing theories as coexistent incompatibilities. It is *The Kingdom*, Carrère suggests, that has the sole purpose of not only keeping him aware of

---

7. Carrère, *The Kingdom*, 196.
8. Carrère, *The Kingdom*, 197; emphasis is mine.
9. Carrère, *The Kingdom*, 213.
10. Carrère, *The Kingdom*, 213.

ambiguity but also accountable to provisionality, a reminder that he could be wrong.

What an interesting approach to data collection. Carrère is not seeking to convince through argument, but rather to hold himself accountable. To unearth his biases and expose their provisionality. And, given his time and place, to posit *The Kingdom* as an ambiguous text for his readers who might have forgotten that their own narrativizing theory is also a provisional construction.

Luke and the Creative Moment

> Yes, I think that Luke mourned James and everything he stood for, although his master declared it obsolete. And perhaps, while mourning, he got an idea. In any event, I'm getting one.[11]

In his actual construction of Luke's story, I learn much about the first-century Mediterranean world, the *Gospel of Luke*, and the role of ambiguity in creative nonfiction. I discover factual events. I stretch my intellect. But I also experience literature as an ambiguous event, which is always a metaphor for how I construct a reality from the lines of resistance that I receive from the world of things.

There is the capital "F" fact that I can only know through Thirdness. There is the encyclopedia and the narrativizing theory that I embody. There is ambiguity, standing in the middle, challenging and violating both code and percept. And there is Carrère creating the world of two-thousand years ago, writing:

> When [Luke] heard Paul bad-mouthing James, the Luke that I imagine—because, of course, he's a fictional character, all I'm saying is that this fiction is plausible—couldn't stop himself from thinking that James was right in a way. Or from thinking that Paul was right when James bad-mouthed him. Does that make him a hypocrite? One of those divided men to whom the Lord does not give himself? A man whose yes tends toward no, and whose no tends toward yes? I don't know. But I do think he's a man for whom the truth always has one foot in the opposite camp.[12]

---

11. Carrère, *The Kingdom*, 278.
12. Carrère, *The Kingdom*, 281–82.

The fiction is plausible. I agree. All fictions that stem from the world of experience are equiprobable. Carrère, in this way, is not writing about Luke, but <<Luke>>. And his relationship, his faith, was not in Jesus, but <<Jesus>>, that cultural unit filled with so much good, beauty, evil, and ugliness. What he teases out of it, of course, is due to *his* narrativizing theory, his tension with hypocrisy, and his continuing acknowledgement of truth's various sides.

Mapping his fiction onto reality, I read Carrère not as the author of *The Kingdom*, but as *The Kingdom's* protagonist. The "I" behind the data, collecting, organizing, and narrativizing a story. I cannot help but ask: Is this really about Luke's plausibility or the narrator's? That question, however, is the question I continually find myself hiding within. How do I choose between this reality and that? How do I embody ambiguity and provisionality and equiprobable realities? How do I judge when skipping from one node to the next in an ever expanding, ever flexible, ever fluid network?

"The historian's job," the Carrère writes, "is to give the society in which he lives the feeling that its values are relative."[13] The academic, especially of the interdisciplinary variety, is to provide the culture within which she lives the feeling of provisionality. Our narratives are not concrete, given, or natural. "I, too, am free to invent provided I say that I'm inventing, and set out . . . the degrees of the certain, the probable, the possible, and—right before the completely excluded—the not entirely impossible."[14]

Is there room for provisionality in the academic world of certainty? Can argument also function ambiguously?

"The program Luke sets himself is that of a historian. He promises Theophilus a field investigation, a report that can be trusted. But then what does he write no sooner than he's stated this intention, starting the very next line? Fiction. Pure fiction."[15] But these are my cultural categories rearing their head, not Luke's, surely. Can that be escaped? Am I not trapped within the horizon of my encyclopedia? No. The answer is always no. Ambiguity allows for the paradox of fictions that shape the world and expand the encyclopedia. I am not trapped. But I am accountable to and responsible for the choices I make in the space of ambiguity. Is not that correct?

And here is the hard admission of any academic wrestling with the truth of the thing that she writes. I don't know. I can think. I can suggest. I can posit. But can I know?

---

13. Carrère, *The Kingdom*, 288.
14. Carrère, *The Kingdom*, 293.
15. Carrère, *The Kingdom*, 339.

"But this isn't a fable by Aesop or La Fontaine," Carrère comments on Luke's parables:

> It's the Gospel. It's the final word on the kingdom: the dimension of life where God's will manifests itself. It would be another thing if it were a question of saying: 'That's what life on earth is like: unjust, cruel, arbitrary, we all know that, but you'll see, the kingdom is something else altogether . . .' But that's not it at all. Luke is saying nothing of the sort. Luke says, 'That *is* the kingdom.' And, like a Zen master after pronouncing a koan, he lets you figure it out for yourself.[16]

Conclusion

As a history student, I had to write a dissertation on a topic of my choice. As I knew almost nothing about history but a lot about science fiction, I chose a topic I was sure to know more about than that entire jury: uchronia. Uchronia deals with fictions along these lines: What if things had happened differently?[17]

The Kingdom stands as an ambiguous reminder of provisionality. "In a nutshell," Carrère writes, "I'm all for reading the Bible as it suits me, as long as I bear in mind that I'm doing just that. And I'm all for projecting myself onto the figure of Luke, as long as I'm aware that I'm projecting."[18] All of us, no matter how cringe-worthy the idea—project our emotion, context, and voice into our various projects. We all set out in our expertise to recount objectively the data, but, in the end, do little more than tell a story wherein the academic—much like Carrère in *The Kingdom*—embodies the "I" of the protagonist. And it is ambiguity that allows us to know that our projection is just that—a projection.

Why is this such an important reminder? Because when approached this way, academia is seen for what it is, a wonderfully world-enriching, but ultimately provisional, accumulation of knowledge. And when viewed as provisional, one cannot help but wonder if perhaps we should not all end our books as Carrère has done, with three simple and humble words: "I don't know."[19]

---

16. Carrère, *The Kingdom*, 361.
17. Carrère, *The Kingdom*, 373.
18. Carrère, *The Kingdom*, 251.
19. Carrère, *The Kingdom*, 384.

5

Mapping the Forest

> Cervantes' text and Menard's are verbally identical, but the second is almost infinitely richer. (More ambiguous, his detractors will say, but ambiguity is richness) ... Menard, a contemporary of William James, does not define history as an inquiry into reality but as its origin. Historical truth, for him, is not what has happened; it is what we judge to have happened.
>
> —Jorge Luis Borges, *Pierre Menard, Author of the Quixote*

Introduction

In the previous chapter, I employed my theory of ambiguity in the work of deciphering the encyclopedia of *The Prague Cemetery*'s protagonist, Simone Simonini. I argued that Simonini represents ambiguity on two levels: one, the ambiguity that he confronts outside of Turin's ghetto, which resulted in the rejection of an alternative reality, and two, the ambiguity that I encountered as a reader when faced with Simonini's *odi ergo sum*. I articulated the role of aesthetic judgment or choice within my theory of ambiguity, which spawned a series of questions: Should I ratify Simonini's local encyclopedia into the universal encyclopedia? If I do, then how does his *cogito* alter my reality? If I do not, then by what rules do I choose to reject it? Are the rules to which I defer constructed, assumed, or given as natural? I claimed, in the end, that choice is both essential to ambiguity and that which maintains a responsible accountability.

The questions taken up in this chapter not only continue my line of inquiry but also explore the entanglement of fiction and reality. The purpose behind this approach is twofold: one, to engage further the possibilities of ordering one's encyclopedia and the way in which choice and provisionality are revealed by ambiguity. And two, to show the ways in which academia, through its theorizations and ideological structures, participates in this ordering. The later argument is neither a critique of objectivity nor a naïve deconstruction of the human and natural sciences. It is, rather, to suggest that *all* knowledge is organized, limited, and idiosyncratic, and, once confronted by ambiguity, provisional.[1] The theories that academics construct and employ in the analysis of the material world are tools for the narrativization of reality. And while it cannot be otherwise, both the tools and the narratives—as well as the material artifacts on which they are based—are temporary stopping points in an ever changing, ever fluid network. What I write today will not hold, for both the encyclopedia and the world are in flux.

The questions that I ask in this chapter then are rooted in Eco's analysis of Simone Simonini in the context of Eco's lectures on the distinction between fiction and reality, and how one might misstep when applying the former to the latter.[2] Filtered through my theory of ambiguity the questions become: What is the difference between a narrative and a theory? Where do they overlap? How does the simultaneity of a narrativized theory further develop my understanding of ambiguity?

By way of a preliminary answer, let me refer you to the epigraph. Jorge Luis Borges writes that Pierre Menard composed "*the Quixote itself*,"[3] and in doing so created something "infinitely richer."[4] Why was it richer? Because it was ambiguous. This richness is similar to Eco's ambiguity-as-information-theory. Whereas Eco might say a given message is high in information (surprise), Borges might claim: "text x is high in richness, which is a measure of its ambiguity." The key is not the connection between Menard's excess and Eco's understanding of information theory, but rather the way in which Borges' short story introduces my concern for this chapter.

After admitting ambiguity into his aesthetic, Borges writes: history is the origin of reality. It is what the community of interpreters—me, you, and everyone else who is responsible for the universal encyclopedia—judges to have happened.[5] History is an arranged or emplotted narrative that forms a reality and then ratifies into a universal encyclopedia. Am I then accountable to history? No. But I am, following from the last chapter, accountable to and responsible for that which I judge—choose—history to be.[6]

To swap out history for narratives is to arrive at this chapter's concern. Or perhaps another way to phrase it would be to say that while history is the

---

1. Cf. Sloman and Fernbach, *The Knowledge Illusion*.
2. Cf. Eco, *Six Walks in the Fictional Woods*.
3. Eco, *Six Walks in the Fictional Woods*, 38.
4. Eco, *Six Walks in the Fictional Woods*, 41.
5. Eco, *Six Walks in the Fictional Woods*, 41–42.
6. Birchall, "Economic Interpretation," 71–87.

a posteriori arrangement of the universal encyclopedia, narratives are much the same for individual and local encyclopedias. Historians argue over, arrange, and analyze the former, while an aesthetics of ambiguity might take up, comment upon, and engage the latter. To keep the two separate is, of course, silly. There is overlap, entanglement, and shared information running through the multi-directional wires of heuristically tiered cultural encyclopedias. But for my purposes, Borges' commentary on Menard's *Quixote* influences this chapter in two, important ways.

It further reveals what Simonini was up to in *The Prague Cemetery*. His meticulous invention, *The Protocols of the Elders of Zion*, was an arrangement of the universal encyclopedia—a history to shape histories. It was a judgment upon an invented happening in order to steer the future course of events. Simonini's narrative was knowledge—arranged and ordered—that was, rather than provisional, certain. Unfortunately, it was largely successful.

And two, Borges' commentary reminds me that Eco's protagonist did not materialize out of thin air. He is, though fictional, a creation spawning from a judgment upon what happened. Eco's research into the historical construction of *The Protocols* mirrors both the arrangement of a given set of cultural units into a narrative and the object of study for an aesthetics of ambiguity—those narratives that, once organized and embodied—shape an equiprobable reality. What I explore in this chapter then is "history as the origin of reality" or the way in which Eco went about collecting scraps of historical data that then set off an aesthetic chain of events.

Eco researched Simonini and the historical construction of *The Protocols* in, among many places, *Six Walks in the Fictional Woods*. From this, he articulated a theory of global conspiracy, which allowed him to write *The Prague Cemetery*, after which—shaped by the data, his arrangement of that data into a theory, and his narrativization of that theory—he espoused another, related idea, that of *Inventing the Enemy*. To be clear, I am not concerned with the timeline in which these events happened,[7] but rather with the way data, theory, and narrative are all entangled. It is difficult for even the most detailed scholar to say where the one begins and the other ends. To do so is to betray an encyclopedic blindness. So much so, it is my contention, that what I take as "reality" is more often, if not always, a narrativized theory shaping my aesthetic judgments. This is not a reversion to concept making the world or semiotics over against embodiment, but rather an admission that the world of things (lines of resistance) and the world of

---

7. Why? Because the timeline of publication is different from Italy to America. Not only that, but because *Narrativizing Theories* relies upon distended reception as espoused in my work, *Sigurd's Lament*, 42–60 and 199–214.

ideas (encyclopedias comprised of cultural units) are so deeply entangled that they are nearly impossible to detangle.[8] As Eco writes it, there is:

> an astronomic infinity of books, each of which straddles different worlds, and stories that some have considered to be true will be seen as fictitious by others ... So the *frisson* with which we perceive the ambiguous confines between fiction and reality is not only equal to the one that seizes us when faced with the books written by angels, but also to that which should seize us when faced with the series of books that represent, authoritatively, the real world.[9]

I am struck equally by the ambiguity of reality when confronted by fiction and history alike.[10] The way in which I arrange reality and understand it through a cultural encyclopedia is neither natural nor a simple matter of facts—a conclusion that I can draw only through ambiguity and the liminality of the skinscape.

To answer my questions before more fully exploring the answers then, the difference between theory and narrative is that the former, in an ongoing process, arranges the latter. Theory and narrative overlap in that the process of ordering and embodiment is never a two-way street with a separating median, but an entangled, overlying network that is dynamic, connected, and simultaneous. I intuit, order, and narrativize in a tangled jumble of simultaneity. And it is that very simultaneity that allows me not only to account for ambiguity in "real time" but also to recognize my judgments as provisional. Though simultaneity and the space of ambiguity that allows for reflection might, at first glance, be at odds—they are not. For, as previously stated, the space of ambiguity, the detangling of simultaneity to account for potentialities, is at the speed of cognition. Or, as Eco might say (referencing Peirce and Calvino), abduction or conjecture is a quick, nimble, and light negotiation.

Eco's novels are the matter to his theories as encyclopedia or cultural units. His theories and narratives shuttle back and forth in a way similar to the entangled simultaneity of the semiotic and material worlds.[11] Ambiguity exposes the way in which knowledge and realities are constructed and arranged, in so far as the event of ambiguity leads to a state of ambiguity (better understood together as the *process* of ambiguity) in which I can analyze potentialities—or, to put it differently, how an aesthetic of ambiguity emphasizes the provisionality of knowledge and the narrativization of reality.

8. Cf. Raffa, "Eco's Scientific Imagination," 34–49.
9. Eco, *The Infinity of Lists*, 365.
10. Cf. Capozzi, "Preface," xvii–xxv.
11. Cf. Eco on the "aesthetic effect" in *Experiences in Translation*, 93.

Walking in the Woods with Eco

I compared the state of ambiguity to networks, nodes, and glowing paths in a digital landscape. I suggested that my contemporary encyclopedia is analogous to a hyperlinked Wikipedia—fluid, dynamic, and crowd sourced. I referenced GitHub, artificial intelligence, and science fiction. While these might be useful metaphors for an encounter with ambiguity in the digital age, Eco's depiction is vastly different.[12] Overgrown with forking paths and the terror of sublimity, Eco's operative metaphor for ambiguity is the rhizomatic woods in which a reader quests and losses herself before forging her own path. While informed by Gilles Deleuze and Félix Guattari, Eco's rhizome is better understood in reference to Joycean puns and Borgesian labyrinths.[13] The woods are a place of mystery, wit, and abduction, a forest of myths and fables existing in reality but only realized upon a reader entering into its dark and foreboding fecundity. The woods represent the process of interpretation, which includes lines of resistance, abduction, choice, and textual responsibility, even as it remains open to infinite paths, perspectives, and possibilities.

"Woods," Eco writes, "are a metaphor for the narrative text, not only for the text of fairy tales but for any narrative text."[14] There are no straight paths in the forest, for within each wood there are forking trails wherein "everyone can trace his or her own path, deciding to go to the left or to the right of a certain tree and making a choice at every tree encountered. In a narrative text, the reader is forced to make choices all the time."[15] I enter the woods. I find myself confronted with a narrative. And I choose. "Indeed," Eco continues, "this obligation to choose is found even at the level of the individual sentence."[16]

While I am perhaps getting ahead of myself, it is necessary to call attention to the role of choice in a silvan hermeneutic, which, of course, is

---

12. Cf. Hix, "Review: Six Walks in the Fictional Woods by Umberto Eco," 229: "Descartes founded modern philosophy, but he also reinforced it with hylophobia. By assuming that the woods are a place of danger from which one should try to escape, Descartes derives an ethical imperative from the metaphor of travelers lost in a forest who know to stay on a single course because, even if it is not the shortest route, it will eventually get them out. Descartes is terrified by the prospect of being lost in the woods, but Umberto Eco revels in the idea . . . [He] reverses Descartes' metaphor. Eco proposes fiction as a cure to modern philosophy's fear of the woods, so that this book is less a theory of fiction than an apology for it."

13. Cf. Eco, *The Aesthetics of Chaosmos* and Farronato, *Eco's Chaosmos*, 8–31.

14. Eco, *Six Walks in the Fictional Woods*, 5.

15. Eco, *Six Walks in the Fictional Woods*, 6.

16. Eco, *Six Walks in the Fictional Woods*, 6.

never *just* a theory of interpretation. Hermeneutics influences aesthetics, which in turn influences epistemology. If I choose in the woods, then it's a safe bet that I also choose in reality—or in those moments where I am actively arranging my experiences.[17] As I have said, I choose and, by doing so, make history, which is *a* reality.

"To read fiction," Eco writes:

> means to play a game by which we give sense to the immensity of things that happened, are happening, or will happen in the actual world. By reading narrative, we escape the anxiety that attacks us when we try to say something true about the world. This is the consoling function of narrative—the reason people tell stories, and have told stories from the beginning of time. And it has always been the paramount function of myth: to find a shape, a form, in the turmoil of human experience.[18]

There is an uncomfortable parallel here between Borges' history and Eco's fiction. In both cases, the questions are what has happened? How do I order it? And, once ordered, what do I call it? Or, perhaps better, what is true about that which is said to have happened? With "truth," however, I arrive back at the encyclopedia.[19] For a truth or a history or a fiction is only true given a set of contextual rules that are often only discovered after an event by utilizing conjecture. This is the metaphysical situation of which fiction serves as a reminder. Truth is always situated in or contextualized by an arranged and organized encyclopedia.[20]

Whereas the real world is full of forking paths, conjecture points, and cultural encyclopedias that require negotiation in order to arrive at a sense of truth, fictional worlds provide their readers "the comfortable sensation of living in worlds where the notion of truth is indisputable."[21] I know that the companion of Sherlock Holmes is John Watson and that he was injured

---

17. Cf. Varsava, "Umberto Eco, Six Walks in the Fictional Woods," 89: "In short, the first-level Model Reader will attend to what the Russian Formalists called the *fabula* and what we refer to as the story or the natural chronology of events whereas the second-level Model Reader will focus on the *sjuzhet*, i.e., the plot or narrative chronology of the text, and enjoy time spent in the textual forest."

18. Eco, *Six Walks in the Fictional Woods*, 87.

19. Eco, *Six Walks in the Fictional Woods*, 89.

20. Cf. Rafa, "Eco's Scientific Imagination," who, along with Bal, critiques this position as naïve, 166–67: "Eco fails to consider adequately the shared cultural grounds needed to establish limits to interpretation in the first place." While I completely disagree, Eco set out to more clearly address this issue in both *Kant and the Platypus* and *From the Tree to the Labyrinth*.

21. Eco, *Six Walks in the Fictional Woods*, 91.

in Afghanistan while serving as Captain in the Fifth Northumberland Fusiliers. This is a fact that is and always will be true. It is the kind of fact that I can only encounter in fiction.[22]

History is the origin of reality. Fiction provides its reader with indisputable truth. It is from these two conundrums that Eco considers not only the role of the "Total Encyclopedia" in representing reality but also that "the way we accept the representation of the actual world scarcely differs from the way we accept the representation of fictional worlds."[23] In both cases, I employ a set of interpretive techniques that help me find my way in the woods.

But if truth can be taken for granted in fiction, in the world of things, "I must make some difficult decisions about my trust in the community . . . I must decide which portions of the Total Encyclopedia are to be trusted, while rejecting others as unreliable."[24] In the world of aesthetic perceptions, I have to choose, make judgments, and employ provisionality as an operative disposition. For without provisionality, I run the risk of continually circling back to a desired origin point and expiring from hunger.

"What is the moral of this story?" Eco asks:

> It is that fictional texts come to the aid of our metaphysical narrow mindedness. We live in the great labyrinth of the actual world, which is bigger and more complex than the world of Little Red Riding Hood. It is a world whose paths we have not yet entirely mapped out and whose total structure we are unable to describe. In the hope that rules of the game exist, humanity throughout the centuries has speculated about whether this labyrinth has an author, or perhaps more than one. And it has thought of God, or the gods, as if they were empirical authors, narrators, or model authors . . . But some (including philosophers, of course, but also adherents of many religions) have searched for God as Model Author—that is, God as the Rule of the Game, as the Law that makes or someday will make the labyrinth of the world understandable . . . The problem with the actual world is that, since the dawn of time, humans have been wondering whether there is a message and, if so, whether this message makes sense. With fictional universes, we know without a doubt that they do have a message and that an authorial entity stands behind them as creator, as well as within them as a set of reading instructions. Thus, our quest for the model author is an Ersatz for that other quest, in the course of which

---

22. Cf. Eco, *The Book of Legendary Lands*, 440–41.
23. Eco, *The Book of Legendary Lands*, 90.
24. Eco, *The Book of Legendary Lands*, 92–93.

the Image of the Father fades into the Fog of the Infinity, and we never stop wondering why there is something rather than nothing.[25]

The truth of fiction then creates a kind of metaphysical paradox wherein I demand a fictional truth from the actual world in the hopes that an author, too, stands behind the narrative of the world of things.[26] But in the woods—terrifying, foreboding, and unkempt—I must make my own way. For there is no author and I am responsible for my own narrative.[27]

Returning to the forest of *The Prague Cemetery*, the question remains: where is Simonini amongst all these swaying trees, splitting paths, and rhizomatic roots? It is Eco's protagonist that contorts the total or universal encyclopedia in such a way that it plays into the metaphysical desire of narrativizing humans. I want the actual world to be a fictional truth. And even if I do not believe in a divine initial point,[28] I am prone to recognize, and perhaps even defer to, an author or authors who stand behind all things, constructing a universal plot. If nothing else, then I can at the very least abdicate any interpretive responsibilities that I might encounter in a sylvan hermeneutic.

But if reality and fiction blend, and I cannot tell where the one begins and the other ends, and if I utilize the same tools to make sense of both, then how do I make a distinction between the two and remain accountable to the narratival choices that I make? Or, as Eco asks it, "If fictional worlds are so comfortable, why not try to read the actual world as if it were a work of fiction?"[29] I have, along with Borges, already answered Eco's question. I do read the world as if it were fiction. This cannot be helped. Eco agrees,[30] but still articulates—through a detailed analysis of the compiling of *The Protocols*—the numerous ways in which fictionalizing reality can go horribly wrong.[31]

---

25. Eco, *The Book of Legendary Lands*, 115–16.

26. Cf. Raffa, "Walking and Swimming with Umberto Eco," 166.

27. The "I" here is a bit hyperbolic, as authority, tradition, and community all go into the shaping of one's encyclopedia. Cf. Eco, *Six Walks in the Fictional Woods*, 130: "Our perceptual relationship with the world works because we trust prior stories. We could not fully perceive a tree if we did not know (because others have told us) that it is the product of a long growth process and that it does not grow overnight. This certainty is part of our 'understanding' that a tree is a tree, and not a flower. We accept a story that our ancestors have handed down to us as being true, even though today we call these ancestors scientists."

28. Cf. Peters, *Sigurd's Lament*, 42–60 and 199–214.

29. Eco, *Six Walks in the Fictional Woods*, 117.

30. Eco, *Six Walks in the Fictional Woods*, 118.

31. Eco, *Six Walks in the Fictional Woods*, 131–37.

And yet, the infinite trap and relativity of language betray me at every turn. To say that a particular narratival arrangement that sought ratification into the universal encyclopedia is "horribly wrong" is to betray my own ordering of the cosmos. I can neither help it nor consider Simonini's work as reputable. It is between my arrangement and Simonini's that I encounter ambiguity and am forced to choose. Simonini is a tree in the narratival woods. To encounter him is to stumble upon a forking path. Do I set foot on his? Mine? A third? Some kind of blending of the two or three or four? Where does it end? Are there boundaries to this branching forest? What if I stay put, paralyzed by the choice? Is that possible, too, or does it only mean that the Simoninis of the world will choose for me? The circular route through the sylvan is one that Simonini manipulates. He chose a road, set dusty boots upon it, and then claimed that somebody else cleared it, directed it, and compelled his feet. To traverse the trail of universal conspiracy is both choice and abdication.

There are natural and artificial narratives—those that describe events that actually occur and those that *pretend* to tell the truth about the actual universe.[32]

> In fiction, precise references to the actual world are so closely linked that, after spending some time in the world of the novel and mixing fictional elements with references to reality, as one should, the reader no longer knows exactly where he or she stands. Such a state gives rise to some well-known phenomena. The most common is when the reader maps the fictional model onto reality—in other words, when the reader comes to believe in the actual existence of fictional characters and events ... There are, then, many reasons a work of fiction may be mapped onto real life. But we must also consider another, far more important problem: our tendency to construct life as a novel.

And while at first glance, constructing life as a novel appears to critique the mapping of fiction onto reality, it cannot be otherwise,[33] which leads to the question: "How should we deal with intrusions of fiction into life, now that we have seen the historical impact that this phenomenon can have?"[34]

The Protocols is an example of an aesthetics of ambiguity informed by coexistent incompatibilities and implicit religion—the mapping of fiction onto reality. To encounter someone who arranges her local encyclopedia differently and then to analyze the way in which she has organized her

---

32. Eco, *Six Walks in the Fictional Woods*, 119.
33. Cf. Eco, *Six Walks in the Fictional Woods*, 130.
34. Eco, *Six Walks in the Fictional Woods*, 139.

embodied narrative is to move towards understanding the difference of the other while creating an opportunity for ambiguity, which allows for the fluidity and transformation of my own encyclopedia. This approach is all the more important when encountering someone utterly despicable, like Simonini. Not only does it allow me to seek understanding and create instances of ambiguity, but it also helps in establishing the borders or boundaries of the communal encyclopedia. It allows me to ground choice and reveal the rules by which I make judgments. As Eco articulates it, narratival analysis enables me to understand the mechanisms by which fictions shape life, which constitutes a form of therapy against the sleep of reason that generates monsters.[35]

If I can understand how encyclopedias are arranged and embodied, then I might be able to participate in the correction or revealing of the dominant, oppressive, or ill-conceived narratives that shape a shared reality. Ambiguity is always self-reflexive, however, and so every analysis is also a questioning of the self and the rules by which I judge, embody, and analyze. Studying the fundamentalism of others, as Eco suggests, helps me understand my own fundamentalisms better.[36]

In the process of ambiguity—encounter, critique, and self-reflexivity—I am reminded that all knowledge and the subsequent embodiments of that knowledge is a provisional negotiation between fictional arrangements. Nowhere is this better espoused than in Eco's works on translation. It is there that he so often asks: what are the rules by which I communicate across languages or, by analogy, encyclopedic arrangements? If it is true that there are lines of resistance, a hard core of Being that suggests all humans crawl but not a one of them flies, then it is there that "languages should be confronted."[37] Whereas philosophy wrestles with the conundrum of ontology when and if it feels like it, translation must continually face it, which is why translation is a better place to discover the provisionality and negotiation inherent to the aesthetics of ambiguity.

For translators, provisionality and negotiation are a given, a pragmatic reality. While translation re-proposes "to philosophy its everlasting question . . . whether there is a way in which *things go*, independently of the way" languages make them go, translators avoid ontological problems by comparing languages and negotiating solutions that do not offend common sense. "Translators," Eco writes, "simply behave like polyglots, because in some way they already know that in the target language a given

35. Eco, *Six Walks in the Fictional Woods*, 138.
36. Eco, *Turning Back the Clock*, 244.
37. Eco, *Mouse or Rat*, 181.

thing is expressed so and so. They follow their instinct, as does every fluent bilingual person."[38]

I can think of no better way to articulate the navigation of trees—decision points—in the aesthetics of ambiguity. I can, upon encountering the ambiguous, behave like a polyglot by comparing encyclopedias and negotiating outcomes. "We negotiate," Eco writes, "because, if everyone stuck to his own interpretation of the facts, we would go on ad infinitum. We negotiate to bring our diverging interpretations to a point of convergence, if only a partial one, that enables us to deal with a Fact—a thing that is there and is difficult to get rid of."[39]

Two keys to aesthetic negotiation are partiality, what I have been calling provisionality, and the uppercase "Fact." The former is an individual commitment (choice) that what is true today is not tomorrow—that aether can become the fabric of space-time. When I negotiate, I hold my own narratives loosely to arrive at a solution that does not "offend common sense." And it is important to note that common sense does not refer to bourgeois assumptions about culture but to both the instinct of the polyglot and lines of resistance. The latter, lines of resistance or Fact, is a challenge to those who might say there are no facts but only interpretations.[40] If this were so, Eco suggests, then

> negotiation would be impossible, because there would be no criterion that would enable us to decide whether my interpretation is better than yours or not. We can compare and discuss interpretations precisely because we can weigh them against the facts they are intended to interpret.[41]

It is Fact or lines of resistance that leads to an interpretation, which then enters, as a cultural unit, into an encyclopedia. When I encounter someone else's interpreted Fact—or, perhaps, implicit religion—through ambiguity, negotiation begins. And by negotiating the convergence of cultural units, or ratifying them into a more general (individual, communal, universal) encyclopedia, I am reminded that all knowledge is provisional. If Fact begins this aesthetic process, then it also ends it, as unlimited semiosis always tells me something more and not something else. I have learned, in other words, something new about that which confronts me. It is through a recognition of this process that I am able, at more general levels of the

---

38. Eco, *Mouse or Rat*, 182.
39. Eco, *Turning Back the Clock*, 248.
40. Cf. Eco, "Absolute and Relative," 22–43.
41. Eco, *Turning Back the Clock*, 248.

encyclopedia, to judge one against the other. It is there that I am able to reject Simonini and choose a different narrative arrangement. And it is there that I am accountable to the choices I make.

The Composer: Part V
The Article that Ed Wrote and Submitted to his Editor for Review

> Abernathy, Edward. "Martynov's Gift: A Light Too Bright To Bear." *The Telescope*. Accessed on September 19, 2017. https://bit.ly/2D2v7ol.

The Voynich manuscript of The Atlantic fame is an artifact with no meaning. We have it. We can see it. Hold it. Turn it over in our hands and question its existence. But the mystery of its import will forever remain unsolved.

And its antipode?

What if I told you that, once upon a time, there was a musical composition for which we knew its meaning but no longer possessed its artifact? We could not play it. Hear it. Or experience it? But we could know it and that for which it stood.

You would, no doubt, call me a liar, a conspiracy theorist. A man who plays with truth.

Perhaps, yes.

But in the Spring of 1892, as the sun set behind Moscow's Bolshoi Theater, Zuravel Ostrava Martynov conceived of such a thing.

By all accounts, he invented a musical composition that was extravagant in detail, beautiful in scope, and utterly haunting.

That, in itself, is not the mystery—and continued influence—of the Martynov composition.

Toiling away in the winter of 1892, Martynov composed sheet after sheet that, according to his journals, could be played in any order.

His idea was to step onto the Bolshoi's stage, throw his composition into the air, collect it, and then conduct it given the order into which it had fallen.

Martynov invented a composition of entropy.

But why?

"So that," he claimed, "the audience could complete the work. For I refuse to dominate man's guttural drive towards the imaginative."

Many critics of classical music refer to this as apocryphal, a story of doubtful authenticity.

What is not apocryphal what many eyewitnesses claim is that after Martynov's orchestra played what is widely held to be the modern world's most influential composition, he turned to his audience, struck a match, and burnt the only record of that which he had invented.

While the memory and meaning lingered, the artifact could never again be experienced. It was a once-for-all-time performance, a thing tinged with loss—that which defied repetition.

According to the journals of Martynov, those in attendance, and contemporary critics, Martynov's burning was artistic anathema. He was said, upon igniting the flame, to have screamed, "I invent to destroy."

In many monographs, critics still try to explain the meaning of that statement and its relationship to Martynov's performance.

Most are in disagreement.

Some say that Martynov was deranged. Others that he was fighting against the then-burgeoning philosophy of Russian materialism. And still, others claim that it was a political statement against those who were seeking to influence the Tsar against the Jewish population in Moscow.

But I cannot speak to any such theory.

From my own research, Martynov was a kind and intelligent man. He was a composer ahead of his time, influential in his own community.

Nikolayevich Romanov Diletsky, the world's foremost scholar on Martynov, calls Martynov's burning a gift. But to whom? His audience? The musical world? To philosopher's everywhere looking for an easy dissertation on aesthetic theory?

While I cannot answer those questions to the satisfaction of this reading community, what I can say is that Martynov was obsessed with time. To him, music was the ordering of experience's cadence. But it was also an escape from humanity's inevitable march towards death.

Music taught that time and history could be arranged differently. That we could see beyond the horizon.

It was a reminder that starting points are false and should be endlessly interrogated. And that, if understood rightly, Being could be worn lightly, with gaiety even.

So is Martynov's burning a gift? Perhaps. If it is, then it is a gift of choice. For only you can decide what it means.

Martynov died in a Siberian labor camp in the Summer of 1892. He was survived by his daughter and granddaughter, who emigrated shortly thereafter to New York.

It is said that his last words were "From ash to light, I leap." I do not know what that means. But it saddens me to think that such a life was spent in the forges of misunderstanding.

The Enemy that Makes

In one of his most pithy statements on the *The Protocols* and universal conspiracy, Eco writes that the intellectual anti-Semitism of today arose in the modern world.[42] Abbé Barruel wrote in 1797 "to show that the French Revolution was a plot hatched by Templars and Masons, and later a certain Captain Simonini (an Italian) pointed out to him that those who pulled the strings were the perfidious Jews."[43] After that began the polemic about international Jewry, which led to *The Protocols*, anti-Semitism in Russian Tsarists circles, and eventually Hitler. The fuller story is recounted in both *Six Walks* and *The Prague Cemetery* but what is important about this account is Eco's distillation of his narrativizing theory, his self-reflexivity,[44] and the way in which it moves from history, through narrative, and towards the argument that *The Protocols* are still in use today, developing a new, popular anti-Semitism. All I need do is "visit certain racist Internet sites, or take a look at anti-Zionist propaganda in Arab countries, and [I] will see the same old recycling of *The Protocols*."[45]

This rhetorically confuses Eco to no end. If writers like himself, Cohen, and Eisner have, time and again, debunked *The Protocols* by revealing their fictional sources, then why are people still using them to whip up anti-Semitic sentiments? "How can we explain," Eco asks, "this resistance to the evidence, and the continuing perverse fascination of this book?"[46] The answer comes only a few paragraphs later: "It is not *The Protocols* that engender anti-Semitism; it is the profound need to identify an enemy that prompts people to believe in them."[47]

It is the aim of this section to examine that final statement by engaging in a reading of Eco's essay, "Inventing the Enemy."[48] My analysis does not exist in a vacuum and is conducted in the hope of exploring the last vestige of narrativizing theories. What happens, to ask it differently, once the data has been collected and reported, the theory has been narrativized, and the final story has been told? It is my argument that "Inventing the Enemy" is analogous to the ways in which narrative arrangements of cultural encyclopedias are embodied in the world of things. By examining it, I better understand the

---

42. Eco, *Turning Back the Clock*, 314.
43. Eco, *Turning Back the Clock*, 314.
44. The short article is titled, "Are the Italians Anti-Semites?" Eco, *Turning Back the Clock*, 313–16.
45. Eco, *Turning Back the Clock*, 316.
46. Eco, *Turning Back the Clock*, 318.
47. Eco, *Turning Back the Clock*, 319.
48. Eco, "Inventing the Enemy," 1–21.

full process of intuition, cognition, and embodiment, which is continuous, fluid, and dynamic. In an ever-continuing process, I encounter, I arrange, I negotiate, I narrativize, and I embody, even as any of those steps might usurp its place and recycle the process from a new perspectival location.

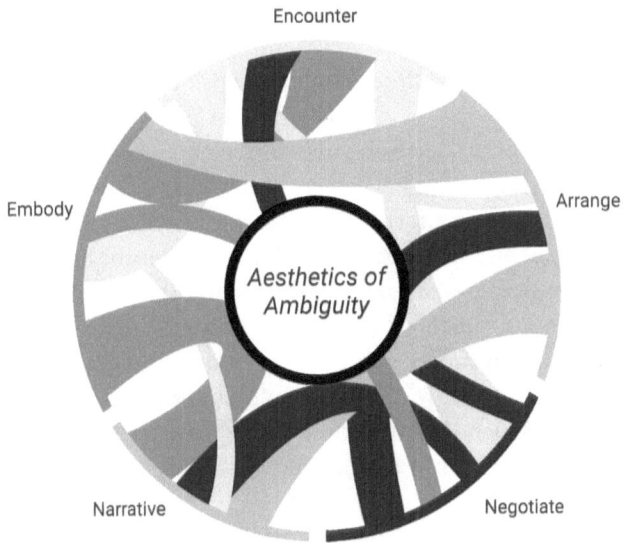

A heuristic diagram that illustrates the ways in which narrativizing theories—as pieces of the puzzle—are non-linear processes rooted in the relationship between thing and interpreter or text and reader. Created by the author and his friend Jeff Appel

Eco's concern in "Inventing the Enemy" is not the process of identifying and naming an actual threat, but the "process of creating and demonizing the enemy."[49] In a convergence of both the semiotic and material worlds, the other is first identified and then connected to various cultural units: <<enemy>>, <<difference>>, or <<foreign>>. The *poesis* of enemy construction defines the identity of the ones who create or narrativize the enemy and also provides them an obstacle against which to measure their system of values. Since <<enemy>> is essential to this creation of identity, if a culture finds itself without one, then it must invent an enemy in order to know itself and what it values—I can place all that I am *not* into the cultural unit of <<enemy>>.

49. Eco, "Inventing the Enemy," 2.

Ambiguity is intrinsically connected to this process in that enemies represent difference, which, in turn, epitomizes foreignness.[50] I could say, thinking back to Part I of *Narrativizing Theories*, that the enemy, to a given cultural encyclopedia, is high in information or surprise and, hence, ambiguity. An enemy will often, if not always, call into question the encyclopedia of those confronting it. Imagine the encounter between a resident and an alien. "You eat that?" the resident might say, in both shock and horror. But in doing so, the resident casts the alien into the cultural units of <<foreign(er)>> and <<difference>>, which is only an interpretant away from <<enemy>>.

While most of this seems harmless, though perhaps exhausting to the newly arrived refugee who has to continually answer questions regarding attire or food or speech, it turns towards Simonini when the other becomes an enemy not because she threatens, but because someone has an interest in portraying her as a threat even when she is not. "The difference itself," Eco writes, "becomes a symbol of what we find threatening."[51] This difference can be depicted in a variety of ways. It is found in the foreign immigrant who speaks and acts badly.[52] It is symbolized in the enemy who must be ugly, as beauty is identified with the good (*kalokagathia*).[53] It is rooted in heresy when one desires to find an enemy within, and even, if not most often, in the lower classes.[54]

The recurring model of <<witchcraft>>, as an example, is a picture painted in a given cultural encyclopedia so that the victim herself admits to doing what she has not done or, at the very least, recognizes herself in the picture.[55] Cultural semiosis creates the enemy, and the victim sees herself reflected in the image. While this might result in a kind of triumphalism when either you or I avoid such "conservative" *poesis*—when we allow for the painting of a truer picture of the refugee or the victim of war—the process of enemy making cannot be escaped. "The figure of the enemy," Eco writes, "cannot be abolished from the process of civilization."[56] Why is that? Because when we do everything in our power not to project the cultural unit of <<enemy>> onto the other, "the image of the enemy is simply shifted from a human object to a natural or social force that in some way

---

50. Eco, "Inventing the Enemy," 3.
51. Eco, "Inventing the Enemy," 3.
52. Eco, "Inventing the Enemy," 4.
53. Eco, "Inventing the Enemy," 5.
54. Eco, "Inventing the Enemy," 5.
55. Eco, "Inventing the Enemy," 17.
56. Eco, "Inventing the Enemy," 17.

threatens us and has to be defeated, whether it be capitalistic exploitation, environmental pollution, or third-world hunger."[57]

Virtuous, perhaps, but it is the *same process* of enemy construction shifted from the individual or community to either a more general and vague population—"flyover country"—or systems of oppression and injustice. For even a hatred of injustice "makes the brow grow stern."[58] Injustice is perhaps better conveyed as <<injustice>>, which suggests that it is neither fixed nor autonomous but rather a fluid category that—much like the objectification of the enemy—can result in the ideological misappropriation of power.

And so, it would seem, I am doomed. I cannot help but create enemies, whether they be individuals, ethnicities, generalized populations, or systemic evils. That which is deemed threatening, via a careful though sometimes unreflective manipulation of the cultural encyclopedia, is necessary for me to solidify my identity. "Know thyself" then is better written as "know thine enemy." But since the construction of enemies is inescapable, the question arises: "Is our moral sense therefore impotent?"[59] How am I am able to judge the conservative construction of the enemy when I am guilty of the same process? The answer, which will not surprise you, is found in ambiguity in general, and Simonini's ambiguity in particular.

Ambiguity allows for a self-reflexive encounter, which leads to both provisionality and negotiation. When I confront the other as ambiguous, I am able to reflect upon my own encyclopedia and cultural units <<difference>>, <<foreign>>, or <<enemy>>. I recognize that knowledge, cultural or scientific, is provisional, which then allows me to negotiate a new cultural unit with different interpretants. A "moral sense" intervenes when one stops pretending that she has no enemies and instead seeks understanding.[60] Confronting that which is different instigates the aesthetic process of ambiguity that results in either a reorganization of the cultural encyclopedia or the rejection of ambiguity as a form of epistemological growth. "Trying to understand other people," Eco writes, "means destroying the stereotype without denying or ignoring the otherness."[61] Simonini is, of course, incapable of understanding. His confrontation with ambiguity resulted in a rejection of the aesthetic process of provisionality and negotiation. His concern was not to destroy the stereotype, but to deepen and manipulate it. Simonini profited by exploiting <<foreignness>>.

57. Eco, "Inventing the Enemy," 17–18.
58. Eco, "Inventing the Enemy," 18.
59. Eco, "Inventing the Enemy," 18.
60. Eco, "Inventing the Enemy," 18.
61. Eco, "Inventing the Enemy," 18.

And yet, Simonini is a complex protagonist. While he rejected ambiguity outside the ghetto in Turin, he presents an opportunity for the reader to either accept or reject ambiguity, too. When confronted with Simonini's otherness, I can seek understanding—not to adopt his views, but to grasp a side of human behavior that I so often expunge as inhuman. Is he my enemy? Yes, in so far as his narrativizing theory is ill-conceived and embodied at peril, but should his hate consign him to the dungheap of inhuman behavior? No. For to wrestle with Simonini's hate in-so-far as it is ambiguous is to understand my own hate, bigotry, and racism better. It is to reconcile with my own fictional narratives that I strive to map onto reality.

This leads me again to the well of judgment and how I choose one fictional representation over another, equiprobable representation. What gives me, you, or us the right to claim one reality over another? Eco, too, found this point essential. In his essay, "Absolute and Relative,"[62] he lays out the various ways in which one can approach judgment or choice within the aesthetics of ambiguity. The answer lies in deciphering, in any given context, the "criteria of truth we are using."[63]

"Consider these statements," Eco writes:

1. I have a stomachache.
2. Last night I dreamed that Mother Teresa appeared to me.
3. Tomorrow it will certainly rain.
4. The world will end in 2536.
5. There is life after death.
6. The sum of the angles of a triangle is 180 degrees.
7. Water boils at 100 degrees Celsius.
8. The apple is an angiosperm.
9. Napoleon died on May 5, 1821.
10. We reach the coast following the path of the sun.
11. Jesus is the Son of God.
12. The correct interpretation of the holy scriptures is decided by the teachings of the church.
13. An embryo is already a human being and has a soul.[64]

---

62. Eco, "Absolute and Relative," 22–43.
63. Eco, "Absolute and Relative," 32.
64. Eco, "Absolute and Relative," 30–31.

These statements are true or false only according to the rules of a given context, the subjectivity of the fact (statements one and two) or the verifiability of the statement (I can check to see if it is raining tomorrow, but I cannot know if the world will end in 2536—even if that statement is true).

For an aesthetics of ambiguity, I am most interested in the rules of a given context.[65] "The sum of the angles of a triangle," by way of example, "is 180 degrees only in the context of a Euclidean system of postulates" or "if the evidence of the Gospels is accepted as historical, the proof of the divinity of Christ would be accepted as such by a Protestant. But this would not be so for the teachings of the Catholic Church."[66] In both cases, as well as the other eleven statements, "it is on the very recognition of various degrees of verifiability or acceptability of a truth that our sense of tolerance is based."[67] I can begin to accept difference because I recognize that there is no all-encompassing context by which I can measure or judge the truths of the other. I must take them as they are, recognize that my own truths are provisional, and then negotiate a way to ratify the event into the encyclopedia.

As I have said, I am responsible for and accountable to ratification or choice. Eco espouses it differently, however. An aesthetics of ambiguity, for him, needs maintain the philosophical position of "holism" in which "every statement is true or false (and acquires a meaning) only within an organic system of assumptions, a given conceptual scheme, or . . . within a given scientific paradigm."[68] These systems, schemes, and paradigms are best situated under the heading of "encyclopedias" and, as such, are necessary to the process of ambiguity. Coexistent incompatibility implies an organizing structure that cannot account for a particular event. Statements are true, false, and meaningful only within a cultural encyclopedia.

"Holists are the first to tell us," given the connection between holism and the encyclopedia, "there are systems that cannot actually explain a series of phenomena, and that *some are far better because they succeed better than the others in doing so.*"[69] If an encyclopedia cannot explain all phenomena, then it is prone to ambiguity, provisionality, and negotiation, which is true of all encyclopedias outside of Babel's library. I can only recognize then, that an other's encyclopedia succeeds through the process of self-reflexivity. Comparison is an important tool in the aesthetics of ambiguity. For to

---

65. I have discussed this at length in *Sigurd's Lament*, 55–58.
66. Eco, "Absolute and Relative," 31.
67. Eco, "Absolute and Relative," 32.
68. Eco, "Absolute and Relative," 33.
69. Eco, "Absolute and Relative," 34. Yes, choice relies upon explanation, which may or may not be a valued criterion. Italics mine.

instigate the process of ambiguity, I need something to encounter—object, other, event—to which I can compare the two or three or four organizing structures that are at play.[70]

While holism follows the line of perspective-based theories in which "reality can be given different perspectives and each perspective matches one aspect of it, even if it doesn't exhaust its unfathomable richness," it does not equate to moral relativism.[71] I must recognize and respect another culture's difference, but I do not have to abdicate my own cultural identity in doing so. I can, through ambiguity, recognize it as provisional, negotiate its borders, and embody the encyclopedia as it exists in fluidity. In doing so, I have not only employed the process of ambiguity, but also judged or chosen one encyclopedia over another, a choice to which I am both responsible and accountable.

Choice. Responsibility. Accountability. Why? Because an absolute does not exist by which I can judge all possible narratives.

> [If an absolute] exists it is neither imaginable nor attainable, but natural forces do exist that support or challenge our interpretations. If I interpret an open door painted in trompe l'oeil as a real door and go to walk straight through it, the fact that it is an impenetrable wall will undermine my interpretation. There must be a way in which things are or behave . . . Death and that wall are the only form of Absolute about which we can be in no doubt.[72]

On the one side then, I have the encyclopedia, ratification, and choice. And on the other, I have Fact with a capital "F." Both limit my interpretations while also suggesting the provisionality of what I know. And, if I can be so bold, it is through these two criteria that I judge Simonini's encyclopedia or system of organization. As I encounter Simone Simonini as despicable, I self-reflexively recognize him as ambiguous. I notice, too, that I maintain a provisional encyclopedia that is in flux and then self-analyze the categories that are in question <<Woman>>, <<Jew>>, and <<Jesuit>>. Based on the cultural units, interpretants, and connections of not only my encyclopedia but a more general encyclopedia (International Human Rights Law)[73] and the requirements of the wall (I have personally met and encountered many women, Jews, and Jesuits), I am able to negotiate a judgment in regards to Simonini's additions to the cultural units in question. In my rejection of Simonini I not only utilize ambiguity to discover and analyze my own

---

70. Eco, "Absolute and Relative," 34.
71. Eco, "Absolute and Relative," 35.
72. Eco, "Absolute and Relative," 43.
73. The United Nations, "The Foundation of International Human Rights Law."

cultural units but also install Simonini's egregious cultural units as part of the complex of interpretants swirling around mine. The latter is not an adoption, but an awareness of the full scope of hate, prejudice, and injustice as it exists in the global encyclopedia.

Conclusion

Writing this chapter in the waning summer of 2017 has been a strange experience. It seems that everyday something is reported in the news that I could have included as an example of negotiating encyclopedias and the way in which a community chooses to either ratify or reject the fluidity of their cultural units. One example of this is the now infamous "Google Memo"[74] sent by a software engineer to the rest of the company at Mountain View. Titled, "Google's Ideological Echo Chamber," it argues, among other things, that "women are underrepresented in tech not because they face bias and discrimination in the workplace, but because of inherent psychological differences between men and women."[75]

Both the memo and subsequent firing of the author resulted in a media frenzy. While some embraced the memo,[76] others outright rejected or critiqued it.[77] Some took issue with the memo, but were then distraught that the employee was fired.[78] Some even sought, critically, to understand its point of view.[79] Others, like David Brooks of the *New York Times* had a different response.[80] According to him, there were four actors in this controversy that made it what it was: 1) the author, James Damore, 2) women in tech, 3) Danielle Brown, Google's diversity officer, and 4) the media. "What we have is a legitimate tension," Brooks writes:

> Damore is describing a truth on one level; his sensible critics are describing a different truth, one that exists on another level. He is championing scientific research; they are championing gender equality. It takes a little subtlety to harmonize these strands, but it's doable. Of course subtlety is in hibernation in modern America. The third player in the drama is Google's

74. Conger, "Exclusive: Here's The Full 10-Page Anti-Diversity Screed."
75. Conger, "Exclusive: Here's The Full 10-Page Anti-Diversity Screed."
76. Brandom, "Google's Infamous Manifesto."
77. Molteni and Rogers, "The Actual Science of James Damore's Google Memo"; and Eggert, "Was Google Wrong."
78. Singer, "Why Google Was Wrong."
79. M. Blake, "The Most Common Error in Media Coverage."
80. Brooks, "Sundar Pichai Should Resign as Google's C.E.O."

diversity officer, Danielle Brown. She didn't wrestle with any of the evidence behind Damore's memo. She just wrote his views 'advanced incorrect assumptions about gender.' This is ideology obliterating reason. The fourth actor is the media. The coverage of the memo has been atrocious.[81]

While I do not side with Brooks in all of his points, I do find it illustrative that, according to him, both sides are describing truths. The question then, when filtered through an aesthetic of ambiguity, is not who is right or has the better truth, but how do these truths negotiate into a more general encyclopedia wherein the community can ratify a fuller cultural unit, though provisional, in regard to <<Women>>, <<Technology>>, and the way in which the one is an interpretant of the other? What is also of interest in Brooks' statement is his assertion leveled at Brown that her critique of Damore's memo is "ideology obliterating reason." Viewed through ambiguity, I can ask: Is that *Fact* or revelatory of Brooks' own encyclopedia?

Judgment is possible within an aesthetics of ambiguity, but it cannot be forced. In the end, we are all responsible for and accountable to the choices that we make when moving through the process of ambiguity. Ratification is typically towards a more general encyclopedia, but local encyclopedias can and do exist that refuse to negotiate and ratify upwards.

So why was the Google Memo such a controversy? Why did it become what it did? Because from nearly every perspective the memo was ambiguous. It provided all parties involved with an opportunity to examine the relevant cultural units in their encyclopedias. It highlighted the provisionality and fluidity of <<Women>>, <<Technology>>, <<Science>>, <<Diversity>>, and <<Anti-Diversity>>, to name a few. It was a cultural conversation about who we are, what we believe, and how we embody our knowledge. It was a negotiation carried out in real time. It was a dialogue about what we allow and disallow in the *Encyclopedia America*. It was an argument over the role of judgment in the aesthetics of ambiguity.

---

81. Brooks, "Sundar Pichai Should Resign as Google's C.E.O."

6

The Finale is Humor

> Perhaps the mission of those who love mankind is to make people laugh at the truth, to make truth laugh, because the only truth lies in learning to free ourselves from insane passion for the truth.
>
> —Umberto Eco, *The Name of the Rose*

Introduction

I HAVE ARGUED THROUGHOUT *Narrativizing Theories* that one aspect of an aesthetics of ambiguity is to follow the trail of choice in any given community. All cultural encyclopedias are arranged into narratives that are embodied in the real world. This is not a one-way street, but an entangled web wherein thing, encyclopedia, and narrative overlap. Oftentimes, like Simonini outside Turin's ghetto, these narratives are confronted by ambiguity. Some of the questions that an aesthetics informed by ambiguity asks is why is this event ambiguous for this particular community? What fictions is it seeking to map onto reality? And is either negotiation or ratification taking place? In answering these questions for Simonini, I have called these "fictions" narrativizing theories, stories that arrange encyclopedias even as the encyclopedia is arranging narratives for embodiment. It is with narrativizing theories and their role in an aesthetics of ambiguity that this chapter is concerned. I argue that Williams' comment in *The Name of the Rose* as found in this chapter's epigraph is essential to understanding narrativizing theories.

But why? Why must we laugh at truth?

Humor is ambiguity in the face of certainty. An aesthetics of ambiguity seeks to uncover the fictions that I map onto reality while also confronting me with the provisionality of my encyclopedia, which implies that its enemy is certainty—a knowledge that is convinced it's arrived at the proper ordering of the universal encyclopedia.

The Composer: Part VI
The Response of Ed's Editor at The Telescope

"This," Gina pointed to her MacBook, "is garbage. I gave you a direct order, from Patrick no less, to write a piece that was accessible, filled with conspiracy. I wanted Dan Brown and instead I got Edward Abernathy and whatever the hell this is."

She took a deep breath. "What do you have to say for yourself?"

I slumped in my chair.

"Do you know how many clicks we got? Do you?"

"I'm optimistic."

"Seven hundred and thirty-two. Seven hundred. That's it. How am I supposed to justify this crap to corporate?"

"Don't. Look," I shifted in my seat, "I got caught up in Martynov's world. It's entirely my fault. I'll take the blame. I'll go to Patrick and—"

"Oh, no you won't. Because you no longer have a job. As of today, I'm revoking your credentials. You went too far this time. *The Telescope* needed a pickup, and you made it a laughing stock. 'Antipode.' 'From which.' Did you forget everything—"

The door swung open. Patrick walked in, graceful as ever. He sat on the edge of Gina's desk, hands in his Westmancott pockets. "Well," he started, "that was an interesting read."

I looked to Gina, a chum amongst whales.

"Patrick," she smiled, "so nice of you to join us. I was just telling—"

"Here's the thing, Ed. I agree with you. With all of it. Martynov was a man ahead of his time. And, quite frankly, one from which we have much to learn. But clicks matter. And do you know why?"

"Advertisers."

"That's right. I don't give damn about our readers or their intellectual stimulation. If they want that, they can read Diletsky. But for us, *The Telescope*, we're not in the business of curious excursuses. We have a standard and an expectation to which we must conform. And if we can't do that, then we fail. You fail."

He had a point. I had mistaken my audience. Ambiguity was a thing I couldn't afford. There was a formula for this kind of thing, and I had forgotten it. Journalism 101.

I stood. "I'll see myself out."

At the door, rising to an unexpected level of stupidity, I turned. "But here's the thing, Martynov instigated a discourse that preceded him. He wanted to get people talking, to offer up their own composition. He wanted his audience to complete his work, to provide their own meaning.

He desired to invent a thing with no beginning, to situate others in the already."

I stepped further into the room before continuing.

"He offered his audience an alternate vision—one that they participated in crafting—one that they could choose over against the prevailing winds of the day. How could I write of Martynov and not emulate him?"

Silence filled the room.

Patrick rose from his corner perch.

Glancing at Gina, he then looked at me. "There's no reason for you to lose your job over this. Not if you don't want to. I'll give you one more chance. Rewrite the piece given the parameters we've set for you, and submit it by the end of the week. You're a writer, after all. Follow directions, and get it done."

I left the office, hopped on the "Q," and walked the final three blocks to the library. I loved the city. The anonymity of it.

The sounds of construction swirled around me as I ascended the steps. I found a table in a remote corner of an empty, echoing hall.

I pulled out my laptop.

The cursor blinked, toying with my anxiety. I couldn't afford any wasted time. I had a deadline to meet.

I closed my eyes, something I often did when writing, and stroked the keys.

The cover-up was easy, I wrote. It took the Tsar little effort to wave his ringed hand and banish a man to Siberia, condemning him to death. The man was Zuravel Ostrava Martynov, a man you've never heard of. He was innocent of his accused crimes, but what did that matter to those in power?

Martynov had played a dangerous game and lost.

Wit and Humor in an Aesthetics of Ambiguity

Ambiguity is many things. And while it would be easy to assume that ambiguity is pregnant with matters both serious and grave—the ground of meaning, choice and responsibility, or even coexistent incompatibility—it's poorer if understood in only those terms. When I confront Simonini as ambiguous, and I run through the process of self-reflexivity, I reveal my own epistemological provisionality, my need for negotiation and ratification. But this does little for Simonini or those hell-bent on a destructive and dogmatic certainty. It does little, in fact, for that liberal scholar who is equally entrenched in her position. Ambiguity cannot force self-reflexivity any more than it can require a healthy awareness of one's own provisionality.

But what ambiguity can do, especially Winkler's strategic and produced variety, is reveal the codes that dominate any ideology. It can accomplish this through wit, humor, and even an epistemological willingness to hold ontologies lightly. Ambiguity as playful—nowhere better explicated than in Eco's essay, "On Truth. A Fiction."[1]—connects to narrativizing theories through Brian McHale's work on postmodernity. For him and Thomas Pavel, ontologies are theoretical descriptions of universes.[2] "An ontology is a description," McHale writes, "of *a* universe, not of *the* universe, that is, it may describe *any* universe, potentially a *plurality* of universes."[3] Narratives are ontologies, too—descriptions of the universe that ambiguity problematizes, confronts, and humorously calls into question.

In the absence of "grounding, narrative becomes a means of building foundations, since storytelling contains its own self-legitimization."[4] While there is no certainty in building "intellectual structures upward from firm epistemological and ontological foundation,"[5] an aesthetics of ambiguity recognizes the line of resistance that is an ultimate no. There is a tension then between postmodernity and an aesthetics of ambiguity. The former claims an inaccessible world, of which there are only interpretations. The latter, lines of resistance to which I am accountable. And yet, there is agreement, too. "Narrative," McHale writes, "recommends itself as a means of building foundations by constructing constructions because storytelling . . . bears within it its own (provisional) self-grounding, its own (local, limited) self-legitimation."[6] An aesthetics of ambiguity claims that, yes, narratives were all we ever had, but that in so far as you or I commit to a particular narrative, we've implicitly committed to a religion of perception to which we are provisionally beholden.

Ambiguity seeks to reveal the narrativizing theories that stem from any choice in the process of perception and admits that this process is inextricably connected to a given culture's encyclopedia, narratives that are all too often taken as real, dogmatic, or certain. But we are not bound by our self-perceived, self-legitimizing narratives. Lines of resistance can tell us no or that, in fact, "that isn't a door but a wall." Ambiguity can also utilize humor and wit to expose the door that lies before us, so beautiful, so elegant, that it confuses my perceptions and manipulates my cultural encyclopedia.

1. Eco, *Meaning and Mental Representations*, 41–60.
2. McHale, *Postmodernist Fiction*, 234.
3. McHale, *Postmodernist Fiction*, 27.
4. Farronato, *Eco's Chaosmos*, 103.
5. McHale, *Constructing Postmodernism*, 4.
6. McHale, *Constructing Postmodernism*, 5.

With humor, I can finally see my narrative for what it is, a coexistent incompatibility. The poets and inventors who utilize ambiguity in this way suggest that humanity "needs to encounter being with gaiety (and hopefully with science too), to question it, test its resistances, grasp its openings and its hints, which are never too explicit."[7]

"Gaiety" here is an important word. How many political meetings or philosophical lectures have you sat through that were bursting at the seams with gravity, weight, and seriousness? I'd imagine that if you're reading this book, then you are familiar with the possibility of a stern life. But in the face of such heaviness—ontologies, epistemologies, ethics—ambiguity treads with a light and cheerful heart. And, in fact, as Eco's protagonist William of Baskerville suggests: "Perhaps the mission of those who love mankind is to make people laugh at the truth, to make truth laugh, because the only truth lies in learning to free ourselves from insane passion for the truth."[8]

I can think of no better way to sum up ambiguity and its ability to unmask those narrativizing theories and self-legitimations that I so desperately embody as the natural order of things. Laugh at truth, approach Being with gaiety, and remember that knowledge is provisional.

Italo Calvino wrote much the same in his Charles Eliot Norton Lectures, *Six Memos for the Next Millennium*, which, as fate would have it, is mine. In his essay on "Lightness,"[9] he suggests that

> Whenever humanity seems condemned to heaviness, I think I should fly like Perseus into a different space. I don't mean escaping into dreams or into the irrational. I mean that I have to change my approach, look at the world from a different perspective, with a different logic and with fresh methods of cognition and verification. The images of lightness that I seek should not fade away like dreams dissolved by the realities of present and future... In the boundless universe of literature there are always new avenues to be explored, both very recent and very ancient, styles and forms that can change our image of the world. And when literature fails to assure me that I'm not merely chasing dreams, I look to science to sustain my visions in which all heaviness dissolves.[10]

---

7. Eco, *Kant and the Platypus*, 56.
8. Eco, *The Name of the Rose*, 491.
9. Calvino, *Six Memos for the Next Millennium*, 3–30.
10. Calvino, *Six Memos for the Next Millennium*, 8–9.

In Calvino's conception, ambiguity is dexterous. It is nimble, quick, and hungry to discover fresh methods of cognition and verification.

He continues, relying on the imagery of Giovanni Boccaccio's character, Guido, who, "so very light . . . vaulted over" a tomb, which was so large:[11]

> If I had to choose an auspicious sign for the approach of the new millennium, I would choose this: the sudden nimble leap of the poet/philosopher who lifts himself against the weight of the world, proving that its heaviness contains the secret of lightness, while what many believe to be the life force of the times—loud and aggressive, roaring and rumbling—belongs to the realm of death, like a graveyard of rusted automobiles.[12]

There have been many such times as these. Times in which wars rage, race divides, and hate trumps reason. In such moments, it is all too easy to despair driven by the sober desire to speak truth to power, unmask ignorance, or rage against the digitized machine. Offense breeds offense, increasing polarization and political flaccidness. Like two, leonine and gray-haired men shouting at the television, the world is angry and yelling—all at once. The fault is theirs or yours, but it's certainly not mine. In fact, let me tell you how wrong you are, have been. I'll spew the fact in a rant that I gleaned from my dark, self-confirming echo chamber. I'll fight the system, which you've exploited for your gain. I'll hide the riches the plebeians steal from my coffers. The line bends, curving back on itself, creating a circle in which the other and the self are identified as the same. Yes, there have been many such times as these. Times in which the right and the left, in their righteous anger, sounded all too similar, living in their graveyards of electronic desperation. The earth burns.

Do I really need more gravity? More obstinacy? Let me convince you with this argument, utilizing these facts, in a somber voice of utter conviction. And yet, ambiguity presents an alternative: the sudden nimble leap against the weight of the world, the secret of lightness embedded in the world's heft—gaiety and joy and laughter in the face of Truth.

Can ambiguity do all of this? Can it be a philosophical aesthetic that laughs at but never mocks Truth and approaches Being with gaiety in a lightness that is at once nimble and fresh? Can philosophers be poets and poets, philosophers?[13]

---

11. Calvino, *Six Memos for the Next Millennium*, 14.
12. Calvino, *Six Memos for the Next Millennium*, 14.
13. Farronato, "A Theory of Medieval Laughter, 123–39.

Laughter defeats certainty. "Either you are Rabelais," Cristina Farronato writes, "or you are Descartes. Either one accepts Order and laughs from within it with the intention of making it explode, or one pretends to reject it so as to restore it in different forms."[14] And yet, the restoration of certainty in different forms is the polis' *modus operandi*. Anecdotal, perhaps, but I once had a professor spend an entire year trying to convince me to adopt his anarchic atheism, playing Descartes to my Rabelais. "Trust me," he could have said, "my narratival certainty is better than 'theirs.' So why not swap 'theirs' out for mine and see what happens?" But what was desperately missing from this scene was the self-reflexive provisionality that ambiguity can bring to any situation. The ability to laugh—through wit or irony—at all ordering that would ask us to swap one certainty for the other without any kind of critical assessment or awareness of the provisionality of knowledge.

The comic then is a form of ambiguity in that it "rises from the violation of a rule," but it does so in such a way that it confronts the Simonini's of the world. For it violates a rule "among those who have absorbed the rule that they also presume it is inviolable."[15] And while much more can be said about humor's connection to ambiguity, this is the key. Gaiety breaks lose my hold on certainty and reminds me, and all of us, that narrativizing theories are provisional. If I can laugh at my own truth, then perhaps I can facilitate the laughter of others. For the language game of wit "is not there for its own sake but involves a cultural critique."[16]

Ambiguity as wit takes aim at culture, it does so to remind me of provisionality. My ideas, beliefs, and, yes, even embodiment might be false. How? Why? Because we all map fictions onto reality. We all live out of narrativized theories waiting to be expanded by ambiguity. But we, yes we, should be wary. "The fact that a big part of our history has been so biased should make us alert and ready to call into question the very tales we believe true, because the criterion of the wisdom of the community is based on a constant awareness of the fallibility of our learning."[17] Beneath ambiguity's large umbrella then, is a wit, lightness, and gaiety—a feathered leap over a stern tomb—that "help us maintain a skeptical distance from the series of delusions constantly offered to humankind."[18]

---

14. Farronato, "A Theory of Medieval Laughter," 128.
15. Farronato, "A Theory of Medieval Laughter," 132.
16. Farronato, "A Theory of Medieval Laughter," 137.
17. Eco, *Serendipities*, 20 and Farronato, "A Theory of Medieval Laughter," 138.
18. Farronato, "A Theory of Medieval Laughter," 139.

Conclusion

There are many examples of literary witticisms that help their readers maintain a skeptical distance. Joseph Heller's *Catch-22* is probably one of the most recognizable in the United States. I would also add as illustrative examples Gabriel Garcia Marquez's *One Hundred Years of Solitude*, Salman Rushdie's *Midnight's Children*, and the more recent *Exit West* by Mohsin Hamid. While all three novelists tackle serious issues—historical repetition, India's partition, or the crisis of the refugee—all three approach their respective topics in such a way that the issue is seen in a new light, from a slanted angle. And yet, the books are riddled with gaiety, wit, and lightness. Who can forget Marquez's flying carpet[19] or Saleem Sinai's nicknames[20] or even Saeed's laughter at Nadia's open hand?[21]

When coexistent incompatibility is approached through the clarifying lens of laughter, it not only takes aim at culture but also conjures provisionality out of the encyclopedia's thick and heavy air. Ambiguity as wit or lightness or laughter is a constant reminder to dogmatists (of which we're all included) that history is a series of delusions about which we should remain skeptical. Ambiguity is many things, and not least among them is the comic, that violation of the rule.

I began this chapter with an epigraph taken from *The Name of the Rose*. Make truth laugh, it said. But that was not the end of the conversation. "Where is all my wisdom?" William of Baskerville continued. "I behaved, stubbornly, pursuing a semblance of order, when I should have known well that there is no order in the universe." Eco's Watson, Adso, later responded to William:

> But how can a necessary being exist totally polluted with the possible? What difference is there, then, between God and primogenial chaos? Isn't affirming God's absolute omnipotence and His absolute freedom with regard to His own choices tantamount to demonstrating that God does not exist?

And to conclude this chapter, I will leave you with William's response: "How could a learned man go on communicating his learning if he answered yes to your question?"[22]

---

19. Márquez, *One Hundred Years of Solitude*, 21–22.
20. Rushdie, *Midnight's Children*, 117.
21. Hamid, *Exit West*, 83.
22. Eco, *The Name of the Rose*, 288.

Excursus Three
Sailing to Sarantium

> They went back out into the fog, untied the mule, began walking again. There was nothing to be seen at all. In front of her the world ended beyond Vargos. It was like walking in a dream, no passage of time, no sense of movement, the slabs of the road cold underfoot, walking away and away.
>
> —Guy Gavriel Kay, *Sailing to Sarantium*

Introduction

I've been calling it an epidemic of co-opting real lives, to do whatever we want to do with them. And as an artist, for my own process, I have a problem with this . . . I'm happier not pretending I now anything about El Cid in Spain . . . He's a Spanish national hero. I'd rather invent a character inspired by him but clearly not identical to him. And then I feel liberated creatively. I steep myself in a period and then I twist it just that little bit to give myself the ethical and creative space that seems to work for me.[1]

Fantasy is a literary genre laden with ambiguity. Often accused of escapism or genre-fiction by the experts, literature of the fantastic has a unique role in the aesthetics of ambiguity. Among its many functions (as if it needed pragmatism), fantasy defamiliarizes to such an extent that a reader can enter into a critique of the semiosphere without bringing the baggage of cultural debate. It fosters an encounter with the self-reflexivity of ambiguity without

---

1. Flood, "Guy Gavriel Kay," https://www.theguardian.com/books/2014/oct/29/guy-gavriel-kay-jrr-tolkien-interview-fionovar-tapesty-the-summer-tree.

appearing to do so. Fantasy's ambiguity, in other words, is oblique but essential to my understanding of coexistent incompatibilities.

In the world of Guy Gavriel Kay's *Sailing to Sarantium*, pagan practices are alive and well in the lands of old Sauradia, on the road to, yet outside the orbit of Sarantium, the heart of the Trakesian empire. But Kasia and her companions, either incredibly brave or profoundly stupid, trudge into the mists on a morning in which the wild things in their wild places stir.[2]

Sold into slavery, Kasia has little choice. She is marked for human sacrifice, and today, on the Day of the Dead, Kasia's owners will sacrifice her to a *zubir* in its Aldwood—the avatar of an old, fierce god. What is left for Kasia but to escape? With the help of two travelers, Crispin and Vargos, Kasia makes her getaway, but the three, evading pursuers, aren't quick enough.

Through the fog and cold and wet, Kasia hears, drawing closer, the voices of those who would offer her to the *zubir*.[3] And so, in a dank, autumn field one fated morning in the sixth-century, Kasia and Crispin and Vargos come face-to-face not only with their assailants but also a power of immense strength in the wild, untamed lands of old Sauradia.

The Repetitions of Fionavar

> In Ygrath the tale is sometimes believed that this world of ours, both here in the southern lands and north beyond the deserts and the rain forests—whatever lies there—is but one of many worlds the gods sent into Time . . . I have no doubt: that some of us are born over and again into various of these worlds until, at the last, if we have earned it by the manner of our lives, we are born a final time into Finavir or Finvair which is the nearest of all the worlds to where the true gods dwell.[4]

Like so many of Guy Gavriel Kay's novels, *Sailing to Sarantium* is an exercise in ambiguity. *Sarantium* is a well-researched, historical fiction that recounts the Byzantine Empire under the reign of Justinian and Theodora.

It is also something else entirely.

Kay is an expert at blending history and fantasy in such a way that deciphering historical truth from Kay's fiction is nearly impossible. In this world, Sarantium is a kind of Constantinople, as Batiara is a kind of

---

2. Kay, *Sailing to Sarantium*, 150.
3. Kay, *Sailing to Sarantium*, 152.
4. Kay, *Tigana*, 418.

Ravenna. The Emperor Valerius can be read as a Justinian, as the General Leontes, a kind of Belisarius. Kay's world plunges into the mysteries of the Mediterranean, maintaining history where necessary, but willingly bending it when appropriate to his narrative. Yes, Leontes (the historical Belisarius), ascends to the emperorship after Valerius (the historical Justinian) is assassinated, but the transformation of antiquity into narrative doesn't end there. A step further into the fictive drizzles of history, Kay poses the question in his novels: How would my chronicles change if I granted my historical subjects their own worldview, without sweeping the unbelievable beneath the rug of post-enlightenment modernity?

By ordering history through fiction, Kay invents a unique sort of ambiguity that only fantasy can re-present. Instead of scoffing at the Sarantine sun god, Jad, *Sarantium* seriously explores the cultural implications of theism. In *Sarantium*, there are no "nature myths," no scientific explanations, and no secular whitewashing. Spirits drift the streets. Souls animate clockwork creations. And pagan gods roam the wilderness, the liminal spaces between the civilized, Jad-Worshiping cultural centers. On the one hand then, there is the wild gods of wild spaces and, on the other, the cultured and sophisticated urban gods of priests and emperors. Taken together, Kay weaves a co-existent incompatibility that not only comments on contemporary practices of religion but also exemplifies the self-reflexivity of ambiguity.

To make one-for-one correlations, however, is the wrong way to read any of Kay's novels. Though they are based in historical research, each one of Kay's fifteen novels are set within a larger multi-verse, which stems from Kay's first published trilogy and primary world, Fionavar, and grapples with the recurrent themes of unquenched desire, historical memory, and the convergence of reality and fiction.

The world of Fionavar, in Kay's subsequent novels, is the echo of a myth that bequeaths each story a Tolkien-esque depth, something that the latter achieved through his rich linguistic background. With Kay, narrative depth is the layering upon layering of story, interconnectedness between narratives, and allusions that span his entire corpus. Each novel, in its own way, alludes to Fionavar, hinting at a cosmos ensconced in a primeval longing that, through repetitions reverberating across multiple worlds, is already but not yet satiated.[5]

The repetitions that haunt Kay's corpus are striking when engaged through an aesthetics of ambiguity. Each novel adds to an ever-growing cultural encyclopedia, rich in meaning, and bursting with fresh interpretants. The primary tale of Fionavar—the "first world" of Kay's invented mythology—is

---

5. Kay, *The Darkest Road*, 425.

encountered again and again across multiple worlds, times, and places, creating a concrete backdrop upon which ambiguity can play.

There are perhaps three levels of depth that Kay's narrative world invents, all of which allow for an encounter with ambiguity. The tension between "history" and Kay's narrativized version of it. The repetitions and reverberations that recur throughout Kay's corpus. And the play between Kay's repetitions, which create a kind of expectation on the part of his reader, and the particularity of each novel's narratival revelation—How will Kay's themes reveal themselves in this story, with this protagonist, in this history? Each level of depth creates the possibility for an encounter with ambiguity between the fictive and the real, between each iterating repetition, and between Kay's invented cultural encyclopedia and the expectations of his readers.

Ambiguity in the Unknown

> Blue moon westering now in the autumn sky. Full as his heart once had been. The white moon, rising from the eastern end of his street, framed on both sides and below by the last houses and the city walls, was a pale, waning crescent. The cheiromancers attached meaning to such things. They attached meaning to everything overhead. Crispin wondered if he could find a meaning to attach to himself. To whatever he seemed to have become in the year since a second plague summer had left him alive to bury a wife and two daughters himself. In the family plot, beside his father and grandfather. Not in a lie-strewn mound. Some things were not to be endured.[6]

In *Sarantium*, Caius Crispus (or Crispin), a mosaicist, is tasked with traveling to Sarantium to dress the dome of Emperor Valerius' new sanctuary (a kind of Hagia Sophia) with a decoration befitting the building's aspirations, an assignment steeped in religiopolitical intrigue—you might even call it, "Byzantine." Questions from the Sarantine court swirl around the mosaicist: Will Crispin paint the image of Jad, Sarantium's god or will he respect the wishes of the iconoclasts, only representing Jad though allusions and natural images?

Long before Crispin arrives in the capital among the maneuvering, backstabbing, and petty jealousy, the mosaicist must first walk to Sarantium,

---

6. Kay, *Sailing to Sarantium*, 65.

down the long "Roman" road that spans the Sarantine Empire. It's on this months-long journey that Crispin hires Vargos to accompany him and discovers, while resting at an inn, the impending sacrificial death of Kasia.

The three escape into the fog on the Day of the Dead, certain they won't live beyond the sun's setting. By midday, they find themselves trapped in a wet field between those that would sacrifice Kasia and the god to whom they would sacrifice her. "The mist swirled about the road, parted for a moment," the story goes, "And in that instant Crispin saw something impossible. A shape from tormented dream, from nightmare. His mind slammed down, desperately denying what his eyes had just told him."[7]

In that cold, orange field, dogs and mules whine. Screams rend the air. And then, to Crispin's horror: There comes "a rumbling sound, as of the earth itself, shaking beneath them."[8] In an instant of ambiguity, Crispin's understanding of the world and the half-world change forever.[9] Reality, as Crispin understands it, falls askew. Confronted with the coexistent incompatibility of a living, breathing power that runs counter to the known world, his mind shuts down. Crispin can't, at least initially, comprehend, because he has no mental category in which to place his experience. For the mosaicist, to see the avatar of a god, a *zubir*, is outside the boundary of the known world.

For reasons only known to the Sauradian gods, the bison god kills Kasia's assailants rather than taking her as a sacrifice and then leads her, Crispin, and Vargos into the Aldwood, the grove of sacrifice. As the three walk behind the *zubir*, Crispin tries to *make* sense of what he's seen and experience, to order reality in a way that is comprehensible and accounts for the stupefying creature that was "more than he could grasp."[10] But in seeking to understand, the path of perception forks. Crispin can either wrap himself in the safety of the known, discounting his own experiences and intuitions, explaining away the unbelievable or he can expand the cultural categories of his pragmatic worldview and connect his experience to the cultural units he already has access to, increasing his interpretants and inventing new understandings across the semiosphere.

Vargos, for his part, also struggles to make sense of what has happened, to reckon with coexistent incompatibility. He turns to Crispin: "How do we worship Jad and his son after this?"[11] How do we, Vargos asks, return

---

7. Kay, *Sailing to Sarantium*, 154.
8. Kay, *Sailing to Sarantium*, 154.
9. Kay, *Sailing to Sarantium*, 156.
10. Kay, *Sailing to Sarantium*, 160.
11. Kay, *Sailing to Sarantium*, 170.

to dogma, order, and practice after an encounter with the unknowable more of the world, knowing that knowledge is provisional and ambiguity is ever-present in the perceptions of life—choices made and not made?

Crispin offers:

> We worship them as the powers that speak to our souls, if it seems they do . . . We do so knowing there is more to the world, and the half-world, and perhaps worlds beyond, then we can grasp. We always knew that. We can't even stop children from dying, how would we presume to understand the truth of things? Behind things? Does the presence of one power deny another?[12]

For Crispin, perhaps, incompatibility doesn't require resolution. Ambiguity reveals the paradox of powers without offering a solution, without presuming to understand the truth of things. But ambiguity is a space that one cannot remain in overlong. The line of resistance eventually pushes back, fogs lift, and choices are made. But the world, after an encounter with ambiguity, rarely stays the same.

The Far Side of Ambiguity

> I'm drawn to writing about times and places on the cusp of transition, of one kind or another. It allows for (creates!) legitimate drama, and characters forced to cope with those transitions (successfully or not). Borderlands have always been, for me, compelling in that way, and in [*Children of Earth and Sky*] I make this explicit: what living on the borders can do to people. And in the novel the borders are shifting—as the boundaries and margins and cultural definitions of our world are in flux. So of course the past has things for us to think about. I'm always wary, though, of proposing clear 'lessons'. I don't want to be that didactic.[13]

On the far side of ambiguity, things are different. Perspectives change. Provisional knowledge is exposed. Cultural units collect invented or altered interpretants. Meanings rearrange. Ambiguity, my confrontation with the

---

12. Kay, *Sailing to Sarantium*, 170.
13. Anders, "Guy Gavriel Kay," https://io9.gizmodo.com/guy-gavriel-kay-shares-his-secrets-for-turning-real-lif-1773635178.

unknown, even at the level of perception, has the capacity to reorganize my commitments, however provisional they might be, in the world. But there is always the option to resist invention, the connecting of two, already but incompatible realities, to keep interpretants in place, or to seek out what is "natural" and ideological over what is unforeseeable and potentially dangerous. Even ambiguity can lead one astray.

Crispin, not long after his encounter with the *zubir* of Sauradia, is presented with an opportunity to reject his encounter with ambiguity by slotting his experience into an already given category, into a tradition that is meaningless—void of content—when he arrives at a roadside chapel. Crispin steps inside, and true to his trade, lifts his head to examine the dome's decoration: "He'd had no warning at all," *Sarantium* recounts, "Crispin took some steps forward . . . a moment later, he found himself lying on the cold stones of the floor, struggling to breathe, gazing up at his god."[14] Crispin's god is no living, breathing *zubir*, of course, but the civilized and civilizing Jad. To see his image in Crispin's time is a rare thing, except for this wilderness sanctuary, Jad's image has been torn down throughout the empire.

> After the Aldwood and the bison . . . Crispin had no barriers within himself, no refuge, and the power of the image above hammered into him, driving all strength from his body . . . He lay flat on his back staring up at the figure of the god: the bearded face and upper torso of Jad massively rendered across virtually the entirety of the dome.[15]

Two encounters then. Two experiences. The one stretching Crispin's cultural encyclopedia beyond its hardback covers. The other fully revealing the existence of multiple chains within the semiosphere—all real, all viable. To Crispin, Jad too is "a figure as absolute and terrifying as the bison had been"[16] Though the *zubir* presented itself in the world or half-world of experience, the other god conveyed itself through art. Both, because of their existence as cultural units, were real, true, demanding, and capable of fostering encounters with ambiguity.

The choice matters, however. Not the choice of one religion or god over against the other, but the choice of ordering and understanding my experiences in relation to the tie between perceptions and the semiotic world. It's difficult, or perhaps quixotic, to assume that I have volition when in it comes to differentiating between perceptions. After all, a rock is a rock is a rock. But even a rock is a cultural unit existing in the semiosphere shaped

14. Kay, *Sailing to Sarantium*, 173.
15. Kay, *Sailing to Sarantium*, 175.
16. Kay, *Sailing to Sarantium*, 175.

and changed by the language I use to describe and understand it. A rock can change me, but I, also, can change the way a rock is understood and acted upon by inventing fresh connections throughout the semiosphere. Choice matters then, not in some value laden way, but as an acknowledgment of what ambiguity reveals and the way in which ambiguity unmasks my perceptions as running parallel to an infinity of coexistent incompatibilities. I can always choose otherwise, but for that, well, I must see myself for what I am and how I function in the world.

Ambiguity in its self-reflexivity examines the structures of the cultural encyclopedia, of the self, of the unknown even in an effort to hold my narrativizing theory in tension with another, equally valid narrativizing theory. Self-reflexivity is non-judgmental in that it doesn't offer a better ordering of the semiosphere but rather an understanding of the way in which the semiotic world, entwined with the world of things, gets ordered or arranged in the first place. Self-reflexivity exposes "the natural way of doing things" and reveals an already otherwise. But self-reflexivity, as strange at it seems, only happens in the places of the in-between, in the perceptions or experiences that catch me off guard. The unknown, the unexpected, and the unlooked-for allows me to turn inward and reflect on the ambiguities, the coexistent incompatibility, of my perceptions.

Laying against the cool stone, the image of his god towering above him, "Crispin felt an aching in his heart for the depths of his own folly, the revealed limitations of his understanding and skill."[17] Ambiguity without self-reflection will always be confined, imprisoned by the ideologies of small men.

> Crispin felt naked before this [image of Jad], grasping that in its own way this work of mortal man in a domed chapel was as much a manifestation of the holy as the bison with its blood-smeared horns in the wood, and as appalling. The fierce, wild power of Ludan, accepting sacrifice in his grove, set against the immensity of craft and comprehension on this dome, rendering in glass and stone a deity as purely humbling. How did one move from one of these poles to the other? How did mankind live between such extremes?[18]

Indeed. Between the experience and the aesthetic, perception and cognition, how do I integrate coexistent incompatibility? I don't think I can. They are inventions of the semiosphere that will forever be sundered, except for, perhaps, the mind that has seen and examined them for what they are, extending acknowledgement and critique and provisionality to both.

---

17. Kay, *Sailing to Sarantium*, 175.
18. Kay, *Sailing to Sarantium*, 175.

Conclusion

> The entirely unexpected will elicit very different responses in people, and the sudden intrusion of the numinous—the vision utterly outside one's range of experience—will exaggerate this, of course. One person will be terrified into denial, another will shiver in delight at a making manifest of dreams held close for a lifetime. A third might assume himself intoxicated or bewitched. Those who ground their lives in a firm set of beliefs about the nature of the world are particularly vulnerable to such moments, though not without exception.[19]

Sarantium is a novel rich in ambiguity. It highlights my confrontation with the unknown and the role that self-reflexivity plays in an aesthetics of ambiguity. *Sarantium* poses many questions, but among them is the ever-important inquiry: How do I reconcile myself to a plurality of religious and philosophical systems that vie for my exclusive and ultimate concern? As Crispin lays beneath a towering image of his god in a state of ambiguity—the lines between his cultural units in constant flux—he can prescribe no answer.

Ambiguity can stretch the cultural encyclopedia. It can foster invention by making strange, new connections across the vast distance between cultural units. It can open up new realities and expose provisional truths. It can even allow for a self-reflection that heightens the awareness of my encyclopedia, though it be water to fish.

But ambiguity can provide no answers.

It can't decipher truth any more than it can tap into "the way things should be." There is only the way things are and the possibilities that emerge from the constant ebb and flow of experience. Ambiguity can show me who I am and how I live, but it can't tell me who to be or how to be it.

And, perhaps, that's the lesson learned from fantasy.

A genre eschewed and disparaged as non-literary, fantasy—an altogether ambiguous genre—takes the semiosphere as it is and cleverly asks me to examine the boundaries of what I know. This examination is not the pushing outward of science fiction that is also a comment on the present moment, but rather an inward turning or self-reflexivity that exposes the conventions of the everyday. Fantasy defamiliarizes, reframes, and stretches the cultural units that I take for granted, whether they be the images I see in the cathedrals of life or the terrifying and raging bisons of experience. Fantasy exposes me to my own ordering while simultaneously holding up before my eyes the ordering of a coexistent incompatibility. What I do with it, however, is up to me.

---

19. Kay, *The Last Light of the Sun*, 463.

Conclusion

When you're around Athene what you think about is new ways of thinking about fascinating bits of knowledge you happen to have, and how you might be able to fit them together to make exciting new knowledge . . . The goddess inclined her head. 'This is an experiment, and this is the best time and place for that experiment. Nothing mortal can last. At best it can leave legends that can bear fruit in later ages.

—Jo Walton, The Just City

HUMANS ARE STORYTELLING ANIMALS. It's a unique gift. Fiction subtly shapes our beliefs, behaviors, and ethics. Brain circuits force narrative structure on the chaos of life.[1] "If you want a message to burrow into a human mind," he writes, "work it into a story."[2] Walter M. Miller Jr. and Thomas Sebok would no doubt agree.[3] Concerned with the science of how stories work on human brains, Gottschall presses the issue: Why do humans still employ story if it is nothing more than escapism? Certainly, evolution would have weeded out narrative, unless, that is, story is perhaps useful and has an explanatory purpose.

Story, when considered as essential to human evolution, defines a particular group as a community, coordinates behavior within that community, and creates powerful systems of incentive. The downside is that narratives—especially when understood in light of an aesthetics of ambiguity—can potentially cause people to behave more decently toward members of their

---

1. Gottschall, *The Storytelling Animal*, xvii.
2. Gottschall, *The Storytelling Animal*, 118.
3. Miller, *A Canticle For Leibowitz* and Beauchamp, "How to Send a Message 1,000 Years to the Future," https://www.theatlantic.com/technology/archive/2015/02/how-to-send-a-message-1000-years-to-the-future/38 5720/.

given community "while vigorously asserting the group's interests against competitors,"[4] a fact that Simonini expertly manipulated.

To take Gottschall at face value suggests that a human cannot embody multiple stories at the same time. I create stories to identify a group, myself within that group, and to clearly demarcate the boundaries of my particular community. I can participate in many social groups—each with claims or obligations that have competing ends—but often, at any one moment, I must choose one claim, one narrative, over another. Identity, in so far as it is shaped by narrativizing theories, is a zero-sum game because it continually articulates coexistent incompatibilities without recognizing ambiguity's provisionality. Identity, when considered as a group embodiment, leads to the "breakdown of modern representative democracy into irreconcilable claims of 'identity politics.'"[5] And, for me, the question is how does one navigate between one irreconcilable claim over against the other? How does one choose? What arrangements of the cultural encyclopedia lead one to embody white nationalism? What narrativizing theory leads one to embody cosmopolitanism? Are these embodiments trapped within their own horizon? Are cultural narratives infinitely at odds? Can an aesthetics of ambiguity open the potentiality of a cultural encyclopedia through its confrontation with other narratives?

Gottschall's book reminds me that I am shaped by stories, that these stories are often in competition, and that art does not always liberate. In his chapter, "Ink People Change the World,"[6] he recounts the biography of Adolf Hitler and his love for Teutonic mythology and its transformation into Richard Wagner's music and operas. It was after seeing *Rienzi*, Gottschall writes, that Hitler became the Führer.[7] In this way then:

> The ink people of [mythologies and] scripture have a real, live presence in our world. They shape our behaviors and our customs, and in so doing, they transform societies and histories . . . Fiction does mold our minds. Story . . . teaches us facts about the world; influences our moral logic; and marks us with fears, hopes, and anxieties that alter our behavior, perhaps even our personalities. Research shows that story is constantly nibbling and kneading us, shaping our minds without our knowledge

---

4. Gottschall, *The Storytelling Animal*, 122.
5. Raschke, *Force of God*, 13.
6. Gottschall, *The Storytelling Animal*, 139–55.
7. Gottschall, *The Storytelling Animal*, 142–3.

or consent. The more deeply we are cast under story's spell, the more potent its influence.[8]

The fictions that we map onto reality are at odds. How do individuals, communities, religions, and even nation states arbitrate one against the other? Throughout *Narrativizing Theories*, I have argued that the answer is ambiguity and the role that it plays in self-reflexively revealing the provisionality of any *one* narrativizing theory.

By all accounts, this book is at its end. I have argued. I have digressed. And I have summarized. And yet, there is more that remains. Injected into each chapter was the short story, "The Composer," which told of Edward Abernathy's research into the events of Zuravel Ostrava Martynov's infamous burning. While I will not comment on the story, I will—as best I can—justify its place within a book that sought nothing more than to articulate an aesthetic theory of ambiguity. To quote Edward: "How could I write of Martynov and not emulate him?"

If ambiguity is that which violates, questions, and challenges to expose the provisionality of any given narrativizing theory, then how could I not play with the expectations—encyclopedic arrangement—that is the monograph? The success or failure of that opening into ambiguity is ultimately up to you, the reader, and the connections that you make across the various parts of this work.

As Martynov desired, so too I.

> Martynov instigated a discourse that proceeded him. He wanted to get people talking, to offer up their own composition. He wanted his audience to complete his work, to provide their own meaning. He desired to invent a thing with no beginning, to situate others in the already.

Perhaps I failed. Perhaps I showed rather than told how I think an interdisciplinary discourse should conduct its business. Perhaps, I am nothing more than a dilettante, writing fiction over against an involved and careful study. Or perhaps, like the epigraph suggests, this is just an experiment that cannot last. I cannot say one way or the other. But I hope to have showed, in many ways and voices, that an aesthetic rooted in ambiguity emphasizes both the provisionality of knowledge and the narrativization of reality. Other than that . . . I don't know.

---

8. Gottschall, *The Storytelling Animal*, 144 and 148.

Bibliography

Achebe, Chinua. *Things Fall Apart*. New York: Penguin, 1994.
Adorno, Theodor W. *Aesthetic Theory*. Edited by Robert Hullot-Kentor. Minneapolis: University of Minnesota Press, 1998.
Anders, Charlie Jane. "Guy Gavriel Kay Shares His Secrets For Turning Real-Life History Into Fantasy." *Gizmodo*. https://i09.gizmodo.com/guy-gavriel-kay-shares-his-secrets-for-turning-real-lif-1773635178.
Aristotle. "On Sophistical Refutations." In *The Complete Works of Aristotle: The Revised Oxford Translation*. Edited by J. Barnes and translated by W. A. Pickard-Cambridge. Princeton: Princeton University Press, 1984.
Asad, Talal. *Genealogies of Religion: Discipline and Reasons of Power in Christianity and Islam*. Baltimore: John Hopkins University Press, 1993.
Atherton, Catherine. *The Stoics on Ambiguity*. Cambridge Classical Studies. Cambridge: Cambridge University Press, 1993.
Atkin, Albert. "Peirce's Theory of Signs." *The Stanford Encyclopedia of Philosophy*. Edited by Edward N. Zalta (Winter 2010). https://plato.stanford.edu/entries/peirce-semiotics/.
Bailey, Edward. "Implicit Religion." *Religion* 40 (2010) 271–78.
———. "Implicit Religion." In *The Oxford Handbook of the Sociology of Religion*. Edited by Peter B. Clarke. Oxford: Oxford University Press, 2011.
Balthasar, Hans Urs von. *The Glory of the Lord*. Vol. 1. Edited by John Riches. 2nd ed. San Francisco: Ignatius, 2009.
Baumgarten, Alexander. *Reflections on Poetry*. Translated by Karl Aschenbrenner and William B. Holther. Berkeley: University of California Press, 1954.
Beauchamp, Scott. "How to Send a Message 1,000 Years to the Future." *The Atlantic*. February 24, 2015. https://www.theatlantic.com/technology/archive/2015/02/how-to-send-a-message-1000-years-to-the-future/385720/.
Begbie, Jeremy. *Voicing Creation's Praise: Towards a Theology of the Arts*. London: Bloomsbury T. & T. Clark, 2000.
Bell, Clive. *Art*. Charleston, SC: CreateSpace, 2015.
Berndt, Frauke. "In the Twilight Zone: Ambiguity and Aesthetics in Baumgarten." In *Amphibolie, Ambiguität, Ambivalenz*. Edited by Frauke Berndt and Stephan Kammer, 121–36. Würzburg: Königshausen & Neumann, 2009.
Berndt, Frauke, and Stephan Kammer, eds. *Amphibolie, Ambiguität, Ambivalenz*. Würzburg: Königshausen & Neumann, 2009.

Birchall, Clare. "Economic Interpretation." In *Illuminating Eco: On the Boundaries of Interpretation*. Edited by Charlotte Ross and Sibley Rochelle, 71–88. Burlington, VT: Ashgate, 2004.

Blake, Aaron. "Kellyanne Conway Says Donald Trump's Team Has 'Alternative Facts.' Which Pretty Much Says It All." WashingtonPost.com. https://www.washingtonpost.com/news/the-fix/wp/2017/01/22/kellyanne-conway-says-donald-trumps-team-has-alternate-facts-which-pretty-much-says-it-all/?utm_term=.ddod838686c9.

Blake, Mike. "The Most Common Error in Media Coverage of the Google Memo: Many Headlines Labeled the Document 'Anti-diversity,' Misleading Readers about Its Actual Contents." *Atlantic.com*, August 8, 2017. https://www.theatlantic.com/politics/archive/2017/08/the-most-common-error-in-coverage-of-the-google-memo/536181/.

Bode, Christoph. "The Aesthetics of Ambiguity." In *Actas Del XII Congreso Nacional de La Asociacion Espanola de Estudios Anglo-Norteamericanos, Alicante 19–22 del Diciembre 1988*, 73–83. Granada: AEDEAN, 1991.

Bode, Christoph, and Rainer Dietrich. *Future Narratives: Theory, Poetics, and Media-Historical Moment*. Berlin: de Gruyter, 2013.

Bondanella, Peter, ed. *New Essays on Umberto Eco*. Cambridge: Cambridge University Press, 2009.

Borges, Jorge Luis. "Pierre Menard, Author of the Quixote." In *Labyrinths: Selected Stories & Other Writings*, edited by Donald A. Yates and James E. Irby, 41–42. New York: New Directions, 2007.

Brandom, Russell. "Google's Infamous Manifesto Author Is Already a Hero to the Online Right." *The Verge.com*, August 7, 2017. https://www.theverge.com/2017/8/7/16107954/google-diversity-memo-antifeminist-manifesto-alt-right-4chan.

Broekman, Jan M. "Firstness and Phenomenology—Peirce and Husserl on Attitude Change." In *Prospects of Legal Semiotics*, edited by A. Wagner and J. M. Broekman, 37–78. New York: Springer Science + Business Media, 2010.

Brooks, David. "Sundar Pichai Should Resign as Google's C.E.O." *New York Times*, August 11, 2017. https://www.nytimes.com/2017/08/11/opinion/sundar-pichai-google-memo-diversity.html.

Brown, Bill. *A Sense of Things: The Object Matter of American Literature*. Chicago: University of Chicago Press, 2004.

Brown, Frank Burch. *Religious Aesthetics*. Princeton: Princeton University Press, 1993.

Bruner, Jerome. *Actual Minds, Possible Worlds*. Cambridge: Harvard University Press, 1986.

Burch, Robert. "Charles Sanders Peirce." In *The Stanford Encyclopedia of Philosophy*. Edited by Edward N. Zalta (Winter 2014). https://plato.stanford.edu/entries/peirce/.

Caesar, Michael. *Umberto Eco: Philosophy, Semiotics, and the Work of Fiction*. Cambridge: Polity, 1999.

Calvino, Italo. *If on a Winter's Night a Traveler*. Translated by William Weaver. New York: Harcourt Brace Jovanovich, 1982.

———. *Six Memos for the Next Millennium*. Translated by Patrick Creagh. New York: Vintage, 1993.

Caglioti, Giuseppe. "Ambiguity." In *New Dictionary of the History of Ideas*, edited by Maryanne Cline Horowitz, 1:53–55. Detroit: Scribner, 2005.

———. "Perception of Ambiguous Figures: A Qualitative Model Based on Synergetics and Quantum Mechanics." In *Ambiguity in Mind and Nature*, edited by Peter Kruse and Michael Stadler, 463–78. Heidelberg: Springer, 1995.

———. *The Dynamics of Ambiguity*. Heidelberg: Springer Science & Business Media, 2012.

Capozzi, Rocco, ed. *Reading Eco: An Anthology*. Bloomington: Indiana University Press, 1997.

———. "Revisiting History: Conspiracies and Fabrication of Texts in 'Foucault's Pendulum' and 'The Prague Cemetery.'" *Italica* 90 (2013) 620–49.

Caputo, John D. "In Praise of Ambiguity." In *Ambiguity in the Western Mind*. Edited by Craig J. N. de Paulo, Patrick Messina, and Marc Stier, 15–34. New York: Lang, 2005.

Carrère, Emmanuel. *The Kingdom*. Translated by John Lambert. New York: Farrar, Straus & Giroux, 2017.

Clarke, Susanna. *Jonathan Strange & Mr Norrell*. New York: Tor, 2004.

Coletti, Theresa. *Naming the Rose: Eco, Medieval Signs, and Modern Theory*. Ithaca, NY: Cornell University Press, 1988.

Cohn, Norman. *Warrant for Genocide: The Myth of the Jewish World-Conspiracy and the Protocols of the Elders of Zion*. New York: Harper and Row, 1967.

Conger, Kate. "Exclusive: Here's The Full 10-Page Anti-Diversity Screed Circulating Internally at Google [Updated]." *Gizmodo.com*, August 5, 2017. http://gizmodo.com/exclusive-heres-the-full-10-page-anti-diversity-screed-1797564320.

Croce, Benedetto. *Aesthetic*. Translated by Douglas Ainslie. Boston: Nonpareil, 1978.

Crowther, Paul. *How Pictures Complete Us: The Beautiful, the Sublime, and the Divine*. Stanford: Stanford University Press, 2016.

Danto, Arthur. *Analytical Philosophy of History*. Cambridge: Harvard University Press, 1965.

De Benedictis, Raffaele. "Il Cimitero Di Praga: The Epistemic Implication between Lies and Reality." *Forum Italicum* 45.2 (2011) 428–50.

Deleuze, Gilles and Felix Guattari. *A Thousand Plateaus: Capitalism and Schizophrenia*. Translated by Brian Massumi. 2nd ed. Minneapolis: University of Minnesota Press, 1987.

Denny, Christopher D. *A Generous Symphony: Hans Urs von Balthasar's Literary Revelations*. Minneapolis: Fortress, 2016.

de Paulo, Craig J. N., Patrick Messina, and Marc Stier, eds. *Ambiguity in the Western Mind*. New York: Lang, 2005.

de Saussure, Ferdinand. *Course In General Linguistics*. Translated by Roy Harris. Chicago: Open Court, 2009.

Desogus, Paolo. "The Encyclopedia in Umberto Eco's Semiotics." *Semiotica* 192 (2012) 501–21.

Dumas, Alexandre. *Joseph Balsamo*. Rockville, MD: Wildside, 2007.

Dunbar, R. I. M., Ben Teasdale, Jackie Thompson, Felix Budelmann, Sophie Duncan, Evert van Emde Boas, and Laurie Maguire, "Emotional Arousal When Watching Drama Increases Pain Threshold and Social Bonding." *Royal Society Open Science* 3.9 (2016) 160–288.

Dunn, Mary. "What Really Happened: Radical Empiricism and the Historian of Religion." *Journal of the American Academy of Religion* 84 (2016) 881–902.
Eagleton, Terry. *The Ideology of the Aesthetic*. New York: Blackwell, 1991.
Eco, Umberto. *The Aesthetics of Thomas Aquinas*. Translated by Hugh Bredin. Cambridge: Harvard University Press, 1988.
———. *Apocalypse Postponed*. Edited by Robert Lumley. Perspectives. Bloomington: Indiana University Press, 2000.
———. *Art and Beauty in the Middle Ages*. Translated by Hugh Bredin. New Haven: Yale University Press, 1986.
———. *The Book of Legendary Lands*. Translated by Alastair McEwen. New York: Rizzoli Ex Libris, 2013.
———. *Experiences in Translation*. Translated by Alastair McEwen. Toronto: University of Toronto Press, 2008.
———. "Dictionary and Encyclopedia." *New Literary History* 15 (2014) 255–71.
———. *From the Tree to the Labyrinth: Historical Studies on the Sign and Interpretation*. Translated by Anthony Oldcorn. Cambridge: Harvard University Press, 2014.
———, ed. *History of Beauty*. Translated by Alastair McEwen. New York: Rizzoli, 2004. Reprinted, 2010.
———. *The Infinity of Lists: An Illustrated Essay*. Translated by Alastair McEwen. New York: Rizzoli, 2009.
———. *Inventing the Enemy: And Other Occasional Writings*. Translated by Richard Dixon. Boston: Houghton Mifflin Harcourt, 2012.
———. *Kant and the Platypus: Essays on Language and Cognition*. Translated by Alastair McEwen. New York: Harcourt Brace, 2000.
———. *The Limits of Interpretation*. Advances in Semiotics. Bloomington: Indiana University Press, 1990.
———. *Mouse or Rat? Translation as Negotiation*. London: Weidenfeld & Nicolson, 2004.
———. *The Name of the Rose*. Translated by William Weaver. 1983. Reprint, New York: Harvest, 1994.
———. "On the Possibility of Generating Aesthetic Messages in an Edenic Language." In *The Role of the Reader: Explorations in the Semiotics of Texts*, 90–104. Advances in Semiotics. Bloomington: Indiana University Press, 1979.
———, ed. *On Ugliness*. Translated by Alastair McEwen. New York: Rizzoli, 2011.
———. *The Open Work*. Translated by Anna Cancogni. Cambridge: Harvard University Press, 1989.
———. *The Prague Cemetery*. Translated by Richard Dixon. Boston: Houghton Mifflin Harcourt, 2011.
———. *The Role of the Reader: Explorations in the Semiotics of Texts*. Advances in Semiotics. Bloomington: Indiana University Press, 1984.
———. *Semiotics and the Philosophy of Language*. Advances in Semiotics. Bloomington: Indiana University Press, 1986.
———. "Sign." In *Encyclopedic Dictionary of Semiotics: Tome 2*. Edited by Thomas A. Sebeok. New York: Mouton de Gruyter, 1994.
———. *Six Walks in the Fictional Woods*. Charles Elliott Norton Lectures 1993. Cambridge: Harvard University Press, 1994.
———. *A Theory of Semiotics*. Advances in Semiotics. Bloomington: Indiana University Press, 1979.

———. *Turning Back the Clock: Hot Wars and Media Populism*. Translated by Alastair McEwen. New York: Harcourt, 2007.
Eco, Umberto, and Costantino Marmo, eds. *On the Medieval Theory of Signs*. Foundations of Semiotics 21. Philadelphia: Benjamins, 1989.
Eco, Umberto, and David Robey. *The Aesthetics of Chaosmos: The Middle Ages of James Joyce*. Translated by Ellen Esrock. Cambridge: Harvard University Press, 1989.
Eco, Umberto, Jonathan Culler, Richard Rorty, and Christine Brooke-Rose. *Interpretation and Overinterpretation*. Edited by Stefan Collini. Cambridge: Cambridge University Press, 1992.
Eco, Umberto, and Thomas A. Sebeok, eds. *The Sign of Three: Dupin, Holmes, Peirce*. Advances in Semiotics. Bloomington: Indiana University Press, 1988.
Eggert, Nalina. "Was Google Wrong to Fire James Damore after Memo Controversy?" *BBC.com*, August 9, 2017. http://www.bbc.com/news/world-40865261.
Eisner, Will, and Umberto Eco. *The Plot: The Secret Story of The Protocols of the Elders of Zion*. New York: Norton, 2006.
Empson, William. *Seven Types of Ambiguity*. New York: New Directions, 1966.
Farronato, Cristina. *Eco's Chaosmos: From the Middle Ages to Postmodernity*. Toronto: University of Toronto Press, 2004.
Fenoglio, Paolo. "Preface to the Italian Edition." In *The Dynamics of Ambiguity*. By Guiseppe Caglioti. Heidelberg: Springer Science & Business Media, 2012.
Fish, Stanley. "Is There a Text in This Class?" In *The Stanley Fish Reader*. Edited by H. Aram Veeser. Malden, MA: Blackwell, 1999.
Flood, Alison. "Guy Gavriel Kay: 'I Learned a Lot about False Starts from JRR Tolkien.'" *The Guardian*, Oct. 29, 2014. https://www.theguardian.com/books/2014/oct/29/guy-gavriel-kay-jrr-tolkien-interview-fionovar-tapesty-the-summer-tree.
Francese, Joseph. "Eco's Poetics of 'The Model Reader.'" *Forum Italicum* 37.1 (2003) 161–83.
Francis, Philip Salim. *When Art Disrupts Religion: Aesthetic Experience and the Evangelical Mind*. Oxford: Oxford University Press, 2017.
Gamboni, Dario. *Potential Images: Ambiguity and Indeterminacy in Modern Art*. London: Reaktion, 2002.
Garcia, Anca Andriescu. "Inventing the Enemy. When Propaganda Becomes History." *Acta Universitatis Sapientiae, Philologica* 5.1 (January 1, 2013). doi:10.2478/ausp-2014-0005.
Garcia-Rivera, Alejandro R. *The Community of the Beautiful: A Theological Aesthetics*. Michael Glazier Book. Collegeville, MN: Liturgical, 1999.
Geertz, Clifford. *The Interpretation of Cultures: Selected Essays*. New York: Basic, 1973.
Gill, Christopher, trans. *Marcus Aurelius: Meditations, Books 1–6*. Clarendon Later Ancient Philosophers. Oxford: Oxford University Press, 2013.
Gleick, James. *The Information: A History, A Theory, A Flood*. New York: Vintage, 2012.
———. *Time Travel: A History*. New York: Pantheon, 2016.
Gleiser, Marcelo. *The Island of Knowledge: The Limits of Science and the Search for Meaning*. New York: Basic, 2014.
Goldstein, Rebecca Newberger. "The Deadliest Hoax: Umberto Eco's Novel Explores the Twisted History of 'The Protocols of the Elders of Zion.'" *The New York Times Books Review*, November 20, 2011. http://www.nytimes.com/2011/11/20/books/review/the-prague-cemetery-by-umberto-eco-book-review.html?mcubz=2/.

Gottschall, Jonathan. *The Storytelling Animal: How Stories Make Us Human*. New York: Marines, 2012.
Greene, Brian. *The Elegant Universe: Superstrings, Hidden Dimensions, and the Quest for the Ultimate Theory*. New York: Norton, 2010.
———. *The Fabric of the Cosmos: Space, Time, and the Texture of Reality*. New York: Vintage, 2005.
———. *The Hidden Reality: Parallel Universes and the Deep Laws of the Cosmos*. New York: Vintage, 2011.
Greimas, A. J., and Joseph Courtés. *Semiotics and Language: An Analytical Dictionary*. Translated by Larry Christ and Daniel Patte. Bloomington: Indiana University Press, 1979.
Haft, Adele J. *The Key to "The Name of the Rose": Including Translations of All Non-English Passages*. Ann Arbor: University of Michigan Press, 1999.
Hamid, Mohsin. *Exit West: A Novel*. New York: Riverhead, 2017.
Harries, Karsten. *Infinity and Perspective*. Cambridge: MIT Press, 2002.
Hayles, N. Katherine. *Chaos Bound: Orderly Disorder in Contemporary Literature and Science*. Ithaca, NY: Cornell University Press, 1990.
———. *Electronic Literature: New Horizons for the Literary*. Notre Dame: University of Notre Dame Press, 2008.
———. "Turbulence in Literature and Science: Questions of Influence." In *American Literature and Science*. Edited by Robert Scholnick, 229–50. Lexington: University Press of Kentucky, 2010.
———. *The Cosmic Web: Scientific Fields & Literary Strategies in the 20th Century*. Ithaca, NY: Cornell University Press, 1984.
Heller, Joseph, and Christopher Buckley. *Catch-22: 50th Anniversary Edition*. New York: Simon & Schuster, 2011.
Hegel, Georg Wilhelm Friedrich. *Hegel's Aesthetics: Lectures on Fine Art*. 2 vols. Translated by T. M. Knox. Oxford: Oxford University Press, 1975.
Hix, H.L. "Review: Six Walks in the Fictional Woods by Umberto Eco." *Harvard Review* 7 (Fall 1994) 229.
Hoffmann, Roald. *The Same and Not the Same*. New York: Columbia University Press, 1995.
Hookway, C. J. *Peirce*. London: Routledge, 1985.
Hoopes, James, ed. *Peirce on Signs: Writings on Semiotic by Charles Sanders Peirce*. Chapel Hill: University of North Carolina Press, 1991.
Howard, W. Scott. "Ember Amen." In *Spinnakers*. Boulder, CO: The Lune, 2016.
Hungerford, Amy. *Postmodern Belief: American Literature and Religion since 1960*. Princeton: Princeton University Press, 2010.
Inge, M. Thomas, ed. *Naming the Rose: Essays on Eco's The Name of the Rose*. Jackson: University Press of Mississippi, 1988.
Kant, Immanuel. *Critique of Judgment*. Edited by Nicholas Walker. Translated by James Creed Meredith. Rev. ed. Oxford World's Classics. Oxford: Oxford University Press, 2009.
Kay, Guy Gavriel. *The Darkest Road*. Fionavar Tapestry Book 3. New York: Ace, 2001.
———. *The Last Light of the Sun*. New York: Ace, 2005.
———. *Sailing to Sarantium*. Sarantine Mosaic Book I. New York: Ace, 2010.
———. *Tigana*. New York: Ace, 1999.
———. *Under Heaven*. New York: ROC, 2010.

Kilby, Karen. *Balthasar: A (Very) Critical Introduction*. Interventions. Grand Rapids: Eerdmans, 2012.

Kruse, Peter, and Michael Stadler, eds. *Ambiguity in Mind and Nature: Multistable Cognitive Phenomena*. New York: Springer, 1995.

Kuhn, Thomas S. *The Structure of Scientific Revolutions*. Chicago: University of Chicago Press, 1996.

Lawson, E. Thomas. "Cognition." In *Guide to the Study of Religion*. Edited by Willi Braun and Russell T. McCutcheon. London: Cassell, 2000.

Latour, Bruno. *On the Modern Cult of the Factish Gods*. Durham: Duke University Press Books, 2010.

———. *We Have Never Been Modern*. Translated by Catherine Porter. Cambridge: Harvard University Press, 1993.

Latour, Bruno, and Michel Serres. *Michel Serres with Bruno Latour: Conversations on Culture, Science, and Time*. Translated by Roxanne Lapidus. Ann Arbor: The University of Michigan Press, 1995.

Le Guin, Ursula K. *The Dispossessed: An Ambiguous Utopia*. Reprint Edition. New York: HarperCollins, 2009.

Lozano, Jorge. *El discurso histórico*. Madrid: Alianza, 1987.

Lustig, Joshua. "Skulking in the Sewers." *Open Letters Monthly—an Arts and Literature Review*, November 1, 2011. https://www.openlettersmonthly.com/skulking-in-the-sewers/

Lyotard, Jean-François. "Answering the Question: What Is Postmodernism?" In *Philosophers on Art From Kant to the Postmodernists: A Critical Reader*. Edited by Christopher Want. Translated by Regis Durand, 237–49. New York: Columbia University Press, 2010.

Maczynska, Magdalena. *The Gospel according to the Novelist: Religious Scripture and Contemporary Fiction*. London: Bloomsbury Academic, 2015.

Mahmood, Saba. *Politics of Piety: The Islamic Revival and the Feminist Subject*. Princeton: Princeton University Press, 2011.

Márquez, Gabriel García. *One Hundred Years of Solitude*. Translated by Gregory Rabassa. New York: HarperPerennial, 2006.

Marsden, Victor E. *Protocols of the Learned Elders of Zion*. Bensenville, Il: Lushena, 2014.

McClure, John. *Partial Faiths: Postsecular Fiction in the Age of Pynchon and Morrison*. Athens: University of Georgia Press, 2007.

McHale, Brian. *Constructing Postmodernism*. New York: Routledge, 1992.

———. *Postmodernist Fiction*. New York: Methuen, 1987.

Meisel, Martin. *Chaos Imagined: Literature, Art, Science*. New York: Columbia University Press, 2016.

Miéville, China. *The City & the City*. New York: Del Rey, 2010.

Walter M. Miller Jr. *A Canticle For Leibowitz*. New York: Bantam, 1972.

Molteni, Megan and Adam Rogers. "The Actual Science of James Damore's Google Memo." *Wired.com*, August 15, 2017. https://www.wired.com/story/the-pernicious-science-of-james-damores-google-memo/.

Moore, Alan. *Jerusalem: A Novel*. New York: Liveright, 2016.

Moriarty, Sandra E. "Abduction: A Theory of Visual Interpretation." *Communication Theory* 6.2 (May 1996) 167–87.

Morris, Charles William. *Writings on the General Theory of Signs*. Paris: Mouton, 1972.

Mott, Carrie and Daniel Cockayne. "Citation Matters: Mobilizing the Politics of Citation toward a Practice of 'Conscientious Engagement.'" *Gender, Place & Culture* (June 2017) 1–20. http://dx.doi.org/10.1080/0966369X.2017.1339022/.

Murthy, Nishevita J. *Historicizing Fiction/Fictionalizing History: Representation in Select Novels of Umberto Eco and Orhan Pamuk*. Cambridge: Cambridge Scholars, 2014.

Mukarovsky, Jan. "Standard Language and Poetic Language." In *A Prague School Reader*. Edited by P. L. Garvin. Washington, DC: Georgetown University Press, 1964.

Paden, William E. *Interpreting the Sacred: Ways of Viewing Religion*. Boston: Beacon, 2003.

———. *Religious Worlds: The Comparative Study of Religion*. Boston: Beacon, 1994.

Pavel, Thomas. "Tragedy and the Sacred: Notes towards a Semantic Characterization of a Fictional Genre." *Poetics* 10:2–3 (1981) 231–42.

Peirce, Charles S. *Essays in the Philosophy of Science*. Edited by Vincent Tomas. New York: The Liberal Arts, 1957.

———. "The Fixation of Belief." *Popular Science Monthly* 12 (November 1877) 1–15.

———. "How to Make Our Ideas Clear." *Popular Science Monthly* 12 (1878) 286–302.

———. *Philosophical Writings of Peirce*. Edited by Justus Buchler. New York: Dover, 1955.

Peters, Benjamin John. "Reading Religion: Chivalry in the Alliterative Morte Arthure as an Instance of Cultural Negotiation." *Literature and Theology*, September 2016. doi:10.1093/litthe/frw030/.

———. *Sigurd's Lament: An Alliterative Epic*. Eugene, OR: Cascade Books, 2017.

———. "Telescope + Mirror = Reflections on the Cosmos: Umberto Eco and the Image of Religion." *Zygon* 52 (2017) 343–60.

———. *Through All the Plain*. Eugene, OR: Cascade Books, 2014.

Phillips, Kristine. "Why These Professors Are Warning against Promoting the Work of Straight, White Men." *The Washington Post*, July 16, 2017. https://www.washingtonpost.com/amphtml/news/speaking-of-science/wp/2017/07/16/feminist-scientists-say-citing-research-by-straight-white-men-promotes-a-system-of-oppression/.

Plate, S. Brent. *A History of Religion in 5½ Objects: Bringing the Spiritual to Its Senses*. Boston: Beacon, 2015

———. "Inventing Religious Aesthetics: Word/Image/Body/Other in Walter Benjamin and Gary Hill." PhD diss., Emory University, 1999.

———. "The Skin of Religion: Aesthetic Mediations of the Sacred." *Crosscurrents* 62.2 (2012) 162–80.

———. *Walter Benjamin, Religion, and Aesthetics: Rethinking Religion through the Arts*. Perspectives on Gender. New York: Routledge, 2005.

Plax, Martin J. "On Extremism in Our Time." *Society: New York* 50.2 (2013) 196–203.

Prigogine, Ilya, and Isabelle Stengers. *Order Out of Chaos*. London: Bantam, 1984.

Radford, Gary P. *On Eco*. Wadsworth Philosophers. Boston: Cengage Learning, 2002.

Raffa, Guy. "Eco's Scientific Imagination." In *New Essays on Umberto Eco*, 34–49. Cambridge: Cambridge University Press, 2009.

———. "Walking and Swimming with Umberto Eco." *MLN Bulletin* 113/1 (1998) 166.

Ransdell, J. "Some Leading Ideas in Peirce's Semiotic." *Semiotica* 19 (1977) 157–78.

Raschke, Carl. *Force of God: Political Theology and the Crisis of Liberal Democracy*. Columbia University Press, 2015.

Roberts, Tyler. *Encountering Religion: Responsibility and Criticism after Secularism.* New York: Columbia University Press, 2013.
Robinson, Kim Stanley. *Aurora.* New York: Orbit, 2016.
Ross, Charlotte and Sibley Rochelle, eds. *Illuminating Eco: On the Boundaries of Interpretation.* Burlington, VT: Ashgate, 2004.
Rushdie, Salman. *Midnight's Children: A Novel.* New York: Random House, 2006.
Santambrogio, Marco and Patrizia Violi. "Introduction." In *Meaning and Mental Representation.* Edited by Umberto Eco, Marco Santambrogio, and Patrizia Violi. Bloomington: Indiana University Press, 1988.
Scheffler, Israel. *Beyond the Letter: A Philosophical Inquiry into Ambiguity, Vagueness, and Metaphor in Language.* London: Routledge & Kegan Paul, 1979.
Schilbrack, Kevin. "Religion, Models of, and Reality: Are We Through with Geertz?" *Journal of the American Academy of Religion* 73.2 (June 2005) 429–52.
Seligman, Adam B., Robert P. Weller, Michael J. Puett and Bennett Simon. *Ritual and Its Consequences.* Oxford: Oxford University Press, 2008.
Sennet, Adam. "Ambiguity." *The Stanford Encyclopedia of Philosophy.* Edited by Edward N. Zalta. Stanford: Metaphysics Research Lab, Stanford University, 2016. https://plato.stanford.edu/archives/spr2016/entries/ambiguity/.
Serres, Michel. *The Birth of Physics.* Edited by David Webb. Translated by Jack Hawkes. Manchester: Clinamen, 2014.
———. *Hermes: Literature, Science, Philosophy.* Edited by Josue V. Harari and David F. Bell. Baltimore: Johns Hopkins University Press, 1983.
Sharnick, Mary Donnarumma. "Devious History." *America Magazine*, March 5, 2012. https://www.americamagazine.org/issue/culture/devious-history
Sheehan, Jason. "'Jerusalem' Is Alan Moore's Really Big Book—In Every Way." *NPR*, September 15, 2016. http://www.npr.org/2016/09/15/493003885/Jerusalem-is-alan-moores-really-big-book-in-every-way/.
Shklovsky, Victor. "Art As Technique." In *The Critical Tradition: Classic Texts and Contemporary Trends*, edited by David H. Richter, 775–84. New York: St. Martin's, 2006.
Short, T. L. *Peirce's Theory of Signs.* Cambridge: Cambridge University Press, 2009.
Singer, Peters. "Why Google Was Wrong: Did James Damore Really Deserve to Be Fired for What He Wrote?" *New York Daily News*, August 10, 2017. http://www.nydailynews.com/opinion/google-wrong-article-1.3399750.
Sloman, Steven, and Philip Fernbach. *The Knowledge Illusion: Why We Never Think Alone.* New York: Riverhead, 2017.
Smolin, Lee. *Time Reborn: From the Crisis in Physics to the Future of the Universe.* New York: Mariner, 2014.
Spruyt, Maria. "Umberto Eco's *The Prague Cemetery*: A Game of Double Co-Incidence." *Literator* 36.1 (2015) 4.
Stengers, Isabelle. *Thinking with Whitehead: A Free and Wild Creation of Concepts.* Translated by Michael Chase. Cambridge: Harvard University Press, 2011.
Sue, Eugène. *The Mysteries of the People.* New York: Penguin, 2015.
———. *The Wandering Jew.* New York: Skyhorse, 2013.
Surridge, Matthew. "Between Forgery and Fiction." *Splice Today*, February 21, 2012. http://splicetoday.net/writing/between-forgery-and-fiction
Taylor, Mark C. *Disfiguring: Art, Architecture, Religion.* Chicago: University of Chicago Press, 1992.

Thiessen, Gesa Elsbeth, ed. *Theological Aesthetics: A Reader*. Grand Rapids: Eerdmans, 2004.

United Nations. "The Foundation of International Human Rights Law." http://www.un.org/en/sections/universal-declaration/foundation-international-human-rights-law/.

Varsava, Jerry A. "Umberto Eco, Six Walks in the Fictional Woods." *International Fiction Review* 22.1–2 (June 1, 1995). https://journals.lib.unb.ca/index.php/IFR/article/view/14370/15447.

Vasquez, Manuel A. *More Than Belief: A Materialist Theory of Religion*. Oxford: Oxford University Press, 2010.

Violi, Patrizia. "Individual and Communal Encyclopedias." In *Umberto Eco's Alternative: The Politics of Culture and the Ambiguities of Interpretation*, edited by Norma Bouchard and Veronica Pravadelli, 25–38. New York: Lang, 1998.

Violi, Patrizia. "'The Subject Is in the Adverbs': The Role of the Subject in Eco's Semiotics." In *New Essays on Umberto Eco*, edited by Peter Bondanella, 113–27. Cambridge: Cambridge University Press, 2009.

Violi, Patrizia, and Wendy Steiner. "Ambiguity." In *Encyclopedic Dictionary of Semiotics, Tome 1: A-M*. Edited by Thomas A. Sebeok. Berlin: Mouton de Gruyter, 1986.

Walton, Jo. *The Just City*. New York: Tor, 2014.

White, Hayden. *Metahistory: The Historical Imagination in Nineteenth-Century Europe*. Baltimore: Johns Hopkins University Press, 1973.

Winkler, Susanne, ed. *Ambiguity: Language and Communication*. Berlin: de Gruyter Mouton, 2015.

Zwicky, Arnold M., and Jerrold M. Sadock. "Ambiguity Tests and How to Fail Them." In *Syntax and Semantics*, edited by John P. Kimball, 4:1–36. New York: Academic, 1975.

www.ingramcontent.com/pod-product-compliance
Lightning Source LLC
Chambersburg PA
CBHW032100230426
43662CB00035B/863